THE AWAKENING OF ASIA

THE
AWAKENING
OF ASIA

Selected Essays

by V. I. LENIN

INTERNATIONAL PUBLISHERS

New York

These selections are from V. I. Lenin, *Collected Works*, Progress Publishers, Moscow, and Lawrence & Wishart, London, © by Lawrence & Wishart, 1963-68.

Library of Congress Catalog Card Number: 76-130865

SBN 7178-0298-1

Printed in the United States of America

CONTENTS

INFLAMMABLE MATERIAL IN WORLD POLITICS
Excerpt

The revolutionary movement in various European and Asian countries has latterly made itself felt so weightily that we see before us the fairly clear outlines of a new and incomparably higher stage in the international proletarian struggle.

There has been a counter-revolution in Persia[1]—a peculiar combination of the dissolution of Russia's First Duma,[2] and of the Russian insurrection at the close of 1905.[3] Shamefully defeated by the Japanese,[4] the troops of the Russian tsar are taking their revenge by zealously serving the counter-revolution. The exploits of the Cossacks in mass shootings, punitive expeditions, manhandling and pillage in Russia are followed by their exploits in suppressing the revolution in Persia. That Nicholas Romanov,[5] heading the Black-Hundred[6] land-owners, and capitalists, scared by strikes and civil war, should be venting his fury on the Persian revolutionaries, is understandable. It is not the first time that Russia's Christian soldiers are cast in the role of international hangmen. That Britain is pharisaically washing her hands of the affair, and maintaining a demonstratively friendly neutrality towards the Persian reactionaries and supporters of absolutism, is a somewhat different matter. The British Liberal bourgeoisie, angered by the growth of the labour movement at home and frightened by the mounting revolutionary struggle in India, are more and more frequently, frankly and sharply demonstrating what *brutes* the highly "civilised" European "politicians", men who have passed through the high school of constitutionalism, can turn into when it comes to a rise in the mass struggle against capital and the capitalist colonial system, i.e., a system of enslavement, plunder and violence.

The position of the Persian revolutionaries is a difficult one; theirs is a country which the masters of India[7] on the one hand, and the counter-revolutionary Russian Government on the other, were on the point of dividing up between themselves. But the dogged struggle in Tabriz and the repeated swing of the fortunes of war to the revolutionaries who, it seemed, had been utterly defeated, are evidence that the Shah's bashi-bazouks, even though aided by Russian Lyakhovs and British diplomats, are encountering the most vigorous resistance from the people. A revolutionary movement that can offer armed resistance to attempts at restoration, that compels the attempters to call in foreign aid—such a movement cannot be destroyed. In these circumstances, even the fullest triumph of Persian reaction would merely be the prelude to fresh popular rebellion.

In Turkey, the revolutionary movement in the army, led by the Young Turks,[8] has achieved victory. True, it is only half a victory, or even less, since Turkey's Nicholas II[9] has so far managed to get away with a promise to restore the celebrated Turkish constitution. But in a revolution such half-victories, such forced and hasty concessions by the old regime, are the surest guarantee of new and much more decisive, more acute fluctuations of the civil war, involving broader masses of the people. And the school of civil war is never lost upon nations. It is a hard school, and its complete course *necessarily* includes victories for the counter-revolution, the unbridled licence of the infuriated reactionaries, the savage reprisals of the old government against the rebels, etc. But only incurable pedants and doddering mummies can moan over the fact that the nations have entered this very painful school. For it is one that teaches the oppressed classes how to wage civil war and how to carry the revolution to victory. It concentrates in the masses of contemporary slaves the hatred which downtrodden, benighted and ignorant slaves have always carried within them, and which leads to the supreme history-making feats of slaves who have realised the shame of their slavery.

In India lately, the native slaves of the "civilised" British capitalists have been a source of worry to their "masters". There is no end to the acts of violence and plunder which goes under the name of the British system of government in India.

Nowhere in the world—with the exception, of course, of Russia—will you find such abject mass poverty, such chronic starvation among the people. The most Liberal and Radical personalities of free Britain, men like John Morley[10]—that authority for Russian and non-Russian Cadets,[11] that luminary of "progressive" journalism (in reality, a lackey of capitalism) —become regular Genghis Khans[12] when appointed to govern India, and are capable of sanctioning every means of "pacifying" the population in their charge, even to the extent of *flogging* political protestors! *Justice,* the little weekly of the British Social-Democrats, has been *banned* in India by these Liberal and "Radical" scoundrels like Morley. And when Keir Hardie, the British M.P. and leader of the Independent Labour Party, had the temerity to visit India and speak to the Indians about the most elementary democratic demands, the whole British bourgeois press raised a howl against this "rebel". And now the most influential British newspapers are in a fury about "agitators" who disturb the tranquillity of India, and are welcoming court sentences and administrative measures in the purely Russian, Plehve[13] style to suppress democratic Indian publicists. But in India the street is beginning to stand up for *its* writers and political leaders. The infamous sentence pronounced by the British jackals on the Indian democrat Tilak[14]—he was sentenced to a long term of exile, the question in the British House of Commons the other day revealing that the Indian jurors had declared for acquittal and that the verdict had been passed *by the vote of the British jurors!*—this revenge against a democrat by the lackeys of the money-bag evoked street demonstrations and a strike in Bombay. In India, too, the proletariat has already developed to conscious political mass struggle and, that being the case, the Russian-style British regime in India is doomed! By their colonial plunder of Asian countries, the Europeans have succeeded in so steeling one of them, Japan, that she has gained great military victories, which have ensured her independent national development. There can be no doubt that the age-old plunder of India by the British, and the contemporary struggle of all these "advanced" Europeans against Persian and Indian democracy, will *steel* millions, tens of millions of proletarians in Asia to wage a struggle against their oppressors which will be just as victorious as that of the Japanese. The class-conscious European worker now has comrades in Asia, and their number will grow by leaps and bounds.

In China, too, the revolutionary movement against the medieval order has made itself felt with particular force in recent months. True, nothing definite can yet be said about the present movement—there is such scanty information about it and such a spate of reports about revolts in various parts of the country. But there can be no doubt about the vigorous growth of the "new spirit" and the "European currents" that are stirring in China, especially since the Russo-Japanese war; and consequently, the old-style Chinese revolts will inevitably develop into a conscious democratic movement. That some of the participants in colonial plunder are this time greatly concerned is borne out by the way the French are acting in Indo-China: they *helped* the "historic authorities" in China to put down the revolutionaries! They feared equally for the safety of their "own" Asian possessions bordering on China.

Proletary No. 33,
July 23 (August 5), 1908

Collected Works, Vol. 15

DEMOCRACY AND NARODISM IN CHINA

The article by Sun Yat-sen,[15] provisional President of the Chinese Republic, which we take from the Brussels socialist newspaper, *Le Peuple*, is of exceptional interest to us Russians.

It is said that the onlooker sees most of the game. And Sun Yat-sen is a most interesting "onlooker", for he appears to be wholly uninformed about Russia despite his European education. And now, quite independently of Russia, of Russian experience and Russian literature, this enlightened spokesman of militant and victorious Chinese democracy, which has won a republic,[16] poses purely Russian questions. A progressive Chinese democrat, he argues exactly like a Russian. His similarity to a Russian Narodnik[17] is so great that it goes as far as a complete identity of fundamental ideas and of many individual expressions.

The onlooker sees most of the game. The platform of the great Chinese democracy—for that is what Sun Yat-sen's article represents—impels us, and provides us with a convenient occasion, to examine anew, in the light of recent world events, the relation between democracy and Narodism in modern bourgeois revolutions in Asia. This is one of the most serious questions confronting Russia in the revolutionary epoch which began in 1905. And it confronts not only Russia, but the whole of Asia, as will be seen from the platform of the provisional President of the Chinese Republic, particularly when this platform is compared with the revolutionary developments in Russia, Turkey, Persia and China. In very many and very essential respects, Russia is undoubtedly an Asian country and, what is more, one of the most benighted, medieval and shamefully backward of Asian countries.

Beginning with its distant and lone forerunner, the nobleman Herzen,[18] and continuing right up to its mass representatives, the members of the Peasant Union of 1905[19] and the Trudovik deputies[20] to the first three Dumas[21] of 1906-12, Russian bourgeois democracy has had a Narodnik colouring. Bourgeois democracy in China, as we now see, has the same Narodnik colouring. Let us now consider, with Sun Yat-sen as an example, the "social significance" of the ideas generated by the deep-going revolutionary movement of the hundreds of millions who are finally being drawn into the stream of world capitalist civilisation.

Every line of Sun Yat-sen's platform breathes a spirit of militant and sincere democracy. It reveals a thorough understanding of the inadequacy of a "racial" revolution. There is not a trace in it of indifference to political issues, or even of underestimation of political liberty, or of the idea that Chinese "social reform", Chinese constitutional reforms, etc., could be compatible with Chinese autocracy. It stands for complete democracy including the demand for a republic. It squarely poses the question of the condition of the masses, of the mass struggle. It expresses warm sympathy for the toiling and exploited people, faith in their strength and in the justice of their cause.

Before us is the truly great ideology of a truly great people capable not only of lamenting its age-long slavery and dreaming of liberty and equality, but of *fighting* the age-long oppressors of China.

One is naturally inclined to compare the provisional President of the Republic in benighted, inert, Asiatic China with the presidents of various republics in Europe and America, in countries of advanced culture. The presidents in *those* republics are all businessmen, agents or puppets of a bourgeoisie rotten to the core and besmirched from head to foot with mud and blood—not the blood of padishahs and emperors, but the blood of striking workers shot down in the name of progress and civilisation. In those countries the presidents represent the bourgeoisie, which long ago renounced all the ideals of its youth, has thoroughly prostituted itself, sold itself body and soul to the millionaires and multimillionaires, to the feudal lords turned bourgeois, etc.

In China, the Asiatic Provisional President of the Republic is a revolutionary democrat, endowed with the nobility and heroism of a class that is rising, not declining, a class that does not dread the future, but believes in it and fights for it selflessly, a class that does not cling to maintenance and restoration of the past in order to safeguard its privileges, but hates the past and knows how to cast off its dead and stifling decay.

Does that mean, then, that the materialist West has hopelessly decayed and that light shines only from the mystic, religious East? Now, quite the opposite. It means that the East has definitely taken the Western path, that new *hundreds of millions* of people will from now on share in the struggle for the ideals which the West has already worked out for itself. What has decayed is the Western bourgeoisie, which is already confronted by its grave-digger, the proletariat. But in Asia there is *still* a bourgeoisie capable of championing sincere, militant, consistent democracy, a worthy comrade of France's great men of Enlightenment and leaders[22] of the close of the eighteenth century.

The chief representative, or the chief social bulwark, of this Asian bourgeoisie that is still capable of supporting a historically progressive cause, is the peasant. And side by side with him there already exists a liberal bourgeoisie whose leaders, men like Yüan Shih-k'ai,[23] are above all capable of treachery: yesterday they feared the emperor, and cringed before him; then they betrayed him when they saw the strength, and sensed the victory, of the revolutionary democracy; and tomorrow they will betray the democrats to make a deal with some old or new, "constitutional", emperor.

The real emancipation of the Chinese people from age-long slavery would be impossible without the great, sincerely democratic enthusiasm which is rousing the working masses and making them capable of miracles, and which is evident from every sentence of Sun Yat-sen's platform.

But the Chinese Narodnik combines this ideology of militant democracy, firstly, with socialist dreams, with hopes of China avoiding the capitalist path, of preventing capitalism, and, secondly, with a plan for, and advocacy of, radical agrarian reform. It is these two last ideological and political trends that constitute the element which forms *Narodism*—Narodism in the specific sense of that term, i.e., as distinct from democracy, as a supplement to democracy.

What is the origin and significance of these trends?

Had it not been for the immense spiritual and revolutionary upsurge of the masses, the Chinese democracy would have been unable to overthrow the old order and establish the republic. Such an upsurge presupposes and evokes the most sincere sympathy for the condition of the working masses, and the bitterest hatred for their oppressors and exploiters. And in Europe and America—from which the progressive Chinese, *all* the Chinese who have experienced this upsurge, have borrowed their ideas of liberation—emancipation *from* the bourgeoisie, i.e., socialism, is the immediate task. This is bound to arouse sympathy for socialism among Chinese democrats, and is the source of their *subjective* socialism.

They are subjectively socialists because they are opposed to oppression and exploitation of the masses. But the *objective conditions of China*, a backward, agricultural, semi-feudal country numbering nearly 500 million people, place on the order of the day only one specific, historically distinctive form of this oppression and exploitation, namely, feudalism. Feudalism was based on the predominance of agriculture and natural economy. The source of the feudal exploitation of the Chinese peasant was his *attachment* to the land in some form. The political exponents of this exploitation were the feudal lords, all together and individually, with the emperor as the head of the whole system.

But it appears that out of the subjectively socialist ideas and programmes of the Chinese democrat there emerges in fact a programme for "changing all the juridical foundations" of "immovable property" *alone*, a programme for the abolition of feudal exploitation *alone*.

That is the *essence* of Sun Yat-sen's Narodism, of his progressive, militant, revolutionary programme for bourgeois-democratic agrarian reform, and of his quasi-socialist theory.

From the point of view of doctrine, this theory is that of a petty-bourgeois "socialist" reactionary. For the idea that capitalism can be "prevented" in China and that a "social

12

revolution" there will be made easier by the country's backwardness, and so on, is altogether reactionary. And Sun Yat-sen himself, with inimitable, one might say virginal, naïveté, smashes his reactionary Narodnik theory by admitting what reality forces him to admit, namely, that "China is on the eve of a gigantic industrial [i.e., capitalist] development", that in China "trade [i.e, capitalism] will develop to an enormous extent", that "in fifty years we shall have many Shanghais", i.e., huge centres of capitalist wealth and proletarian need and poverty.

But the question arises: does Sun Yat-sen, on the basis of his reactionary economic theory, uphold an actually reactionary agrarian programme? That is the crux of the matter, its most interesting point, and one *on* which curtailed and emasculated liberal quasi-Marxism is often at a loss.

The fact of the matter is that he does not. The dialectics of the social relations in China reveals itself precisely in the fact that, while sincerely sympathising with socialism in Europe, the Chinese democrats have transformed it into a reactionary theory, and *on the basis* of this reactionary theory of "preventing" capitalism are championing a *purely capitalist*, a maximum capitalist, agrarian programme!

Indeed, what does the "economic revolution", of which Sun Yat-sen talks so pompously and obscurely at the beginning of his article, amount to?

It amounts to the transfer of rent to the state, i.e., land nationalisation, by some sort of single tax along Henry George[24] lines. There is absolutely nothing else that is *real* in the "economic revolution" proposed and advocated by Sun Yat-sen.

The difference between the value of land in some remote peasant area and in Shanghai is the difference in the rate of rent. The value of land is capitalised rent. To make the "enhanced value" of land the "property of the people" means transferring the rent, i.e., land ownership, to the state, or, in other words, nationalising the land.

Is such a reform possible within the framework of capitalism? It is not only possible but it represents the purest, most consistent, and ideally perfect capitalism. Marx pointed this out in *The Poverty of Philosophy,* he proved it in detail in Volume III of *Capital*, and developed it with particular clarity in his controversy with Rodbertus in *Theories of Surplus Value.*

Land nationalisation makes it possible to abolish absolute rent, leaving only differential rent. According to Marx's theory, land nationalisation means a maximum elimination of medieval monopolies and medieval relations in agriculture, maximum freedom in buying and selling land, and maximum facilities for agriculture to adapt itself to the market. The irony of history is that Narodism, in order to "combat capitalism" in agriculture, champions an agrarian programme that, if fully carried out, would mean the *most* rapid development of capitalism in agriculture.

What economic necessity is behind the spread of the most progressive bourgeois-democratic agrarian programmes in one of the most backward peasant countries of Asia? It is the necessity of destroying feudalism in all its forms and manifestations.

The more China lagged behind Europe and Japan, the more it was threatened with fragmentation and national disintegration. It could be "renovated" only by the heroism of the revolutionary masses, a heroism capable of creating a Chinese republic in the sphere of politics, and of ensuring, through land nationalisation, the most rapid capitalist progress in the sphere of agriculture.

Whether and to what extent this will succeed is another question. In their bourgeois revolutions, various countries achieved various degrees of political and agrarian democracy, and in the most diverse combinations. The decisive factors will be the international situation and the alignment of the social forces in China. The emperor will certainly try to unite the feudal lords, the bureaucracy and the clergy in an attempt at restoration. Yüan Shih-k'ai, who represents a bourgeoisie that has only just changed from liberal-monarchist to liberal-republican (for how long?), will pursue a policy of manoeuvring between monarchy and revolution. The revolutionary bourgeois democracy, represented by Sun Yat-sen, is correct in seeking ways and means of "renovating" China through maximum development of the initiative, determination and boldness of the peasant masses in the matter of political and agrarian reforms.

Lastly, the Chinese proletariat will increase as the number of Shanghais increases. It will probably form some kind of Chinese Social-Democratic labour party which, while criticising the petty-bourgeois utopias and reactionary views of Sun Yat-sen, will certainly take care to single out, defend and develop the revolutionary-democratic core of his political and agrarian programme.

Nevskaya Zvezda No. 17,
July 15, 1912

Signed: *Vl. Ilyin*

Collected Works, Vol. 18

THE END OF THE ITALO-TURKISH WAR

Representatives of Italy and Turkey have signed preliminary terms of peace, according to telegraphic reports.

Italy has "won" the war, which she launched a year ago to seize Turkish possessions in Africa. From now on, Tripoli will belong to Italy.[25] It is worth while taking a look at this typical colonial war, waged by a "civilised" twentieth-century nation.

What caused the war? The greed of the Italian money-bags and capitalists, who need new markets and new achievements for Italian imperialism.

What kind of war was it? A perfected, civilised bloodbath, the massacre of Arabs with the help of the "latest" weapons.

The Arabs put up a desperate resistance. When, at the beginning of the war, the Italian admirals were incautious enough to land 1,200 marines, the Arabs attacked them and killed some 600. By way of "retaliation", about 3,000 Arabs were butchered, whole families were plundered and done to death, with women and children massacred in cold blood. The Italians are a civilised, constitutional nation.

About 1,000 Arabs were hanged.

The Italian casualties exceeded 20,000, including 17,429 sick, 600 missing and 1,405 killed.

The war cost the Italians over 800 million lire, or over 320 million rubles. It resulted in terrible unemployment and industrial stagnation.

The Arabs lost about 14,800 lives. Despite the "peace", the war will actually go on, for the Arab tribes in the heart of Africa, in areas far away from the coast, will refuse to submit. And for a long time to come they will be "civilised" by bayonet, bullet, noose, fire and rape.

Italy, of course, is no better and no worse than the other capitalist countries. All of them alike are governed by the bourgeoisie, which stops at no carnage in its quest for new sources of profit.

Pravda No. 129,
September 28, 1912

Signed: *T.*

Collected Works, Vol. 18

REGENERATED CHINA

Progressive and civilised Europe shows no interest in the regeneration of China. Four hundred million backward Asians have attained freedom, and have awakened to political life. *One quarter* of the world's population has passed, so to say, from torpor to enlightenment, movement and struggle.

But civilised Europe does not care. To this day even the French Republic has not officially recognised the Republic of China! A question on this subject is to be asked shortly in the French Chamber of Deputies.

Why this indifference on the part of Europe? The explanation is that throughout the West power is in the hands of the imperialist bourgeoisie, which is already three-quarters decayed and willing to sell all its "civilisation" to any adventurer who will take "stringent" measures against the workers, or for an extra five kopeks' profit on the ruble. To this bourgeoisie, China is *only* booty, and now that Russia has taken Mongolia into her "tender embrace", the Japanese, British, Germans, etc., will probably try to tear off a piece of this booty.

But China's regeneration is making speed nevertheless. Parliamentary elections are about to be held—the *first* in what was a despotic state. The Lower House will have 600 members and the "Senate", 274.

Suffrage is *neither* universal *nor* direct. It is granted only to persons above the age of 21 who have resided in the constituency for at least two years and who pay direct taxes amounting to about two rubles, or own property worth about 500 rubles. They will first vote for electors, who will elect the members of parliament.

This kind of suffrage indicates in itself that there is an alliance of the well-to-do peasantry and the bourgeoisie, there being no proletariat at all or one that is completely powerless.

The same circumstance is evident from the nature of China's political parties. There are three main parties:

(1) The Radical-Socialist Party, which in fact has *nothing at all* to do with socialism, any more than our own Popular Socialists (and nine-tenths of the Socialist-Revolutionaries). It is a party of petty-bourgeois *democrats*, and its chief demands are political unity of China, development of trade and industry "along social lines" (just as hazy a phrase as the "labour principle" and "equalisation" of our Narodniks and Socialist-Revolutionaries), and preservation of peace.

(2) The second party is that of the liberals. They are in alliance with the Radical-Socialists and together with them constitute the *National Party*. This party will in all likelihood win a majority in China's first parliament. Its leader is the well-known Dr. Sun Yat-sen. He is now drawing up a plan for a vast railway network (Russian Narodniks will please note that Sun Yat-sen is doing this *in order that* China may "avoid" a capitalist fate!).

(3) The third party calls itself the Republican League, an example of how deceptive political signboards can be. Actually it is a *conservative* party, backed chiefly by government officials, landlords and the bourgeoisie of *northern* China, which is the most backward part of the country. The National Party, on the other hand, is predominantly a party of the more industrially-developed and progressive *southern* part of the country.

The peasant masses are the mainstay of the National Party. Its leaders are intellectuals who have been educated abroad. China's freedom was won by an alliance of peasant democrats and the liberal bourgeoisie. Whether the peasants, who are not led by a proletarian party, will be able to retain their democratic positions *against* the liberals, who are only waiting for an opportunity to shift to the right, will be seen in the near future.

Pravda No. 163,
November 8, 1912
Signed: *T.*

Collected Works, Vol. 18

CIVILISED EUROPEANS AND SAVAGE ASIANS

The well-known English Social-Democrat, Rothstein, relates in the German labour press an instructive and typical incident that occurred in British India. This incident reveals better than all arguments why the revolution is growing apace in that country with its more than 300 million inhabitants.

Arnold, a British journalist, who brings out a newspaper in Rangoon, a large town (with over 200,000 inhabitants) in one of the Indian provinces, published an article entitled: "A Mockery of British Justice". It exposed a local British judge named Andrew. For publishing this article Arnold was sentenced to twelve months' imprisonment, but he appealed and, having connections in London, was able to get the case before the highest court in Britain. The Government of India hastily "reduced" the sentence to four months and Arnold was released.

What was all the fuss about?

A British colonel named McCormick had a mistress whose servant was a little eleven-year-old Indian girl, named Aina. This gallant representative of a civilised nation had enticed Aina to his room, raped her and locked her up in his house.

It so happened that Aina's father was dying and he sent for his daughter. It was then that the village where he lived learned the whole story. The population seethed with indignation. The police were compelled to order McCormick's arrest.

But Judge Andrew released him on bail, and later acquitted him, following a disgraceful travesty of justice. The gallant colonel declared, as gentlemen of noble extraction usually do under such circumstances, that Aina was a prostitute, in proof of which he brought five witnesses. Eight witnesses, however, brought by Aina's mother were not even examined by Judge Andrew.

When the journalist Arnold was tried for libel, the President of the Court, Sir ("His Worship") Charles Fox, refused to allow him to call witnesses in his defence.

It must be clear to everyone that thousands and millions of such cases occur in India. Only absolutely exceptional circumstances enabled the "libeller" Arnold (the son of an influential London journalist) to get out of prison and secure publicity for the case.

Do not forget that the British Liberals put their "best" people at the head of the Indian administration. Not long ago the Viceroy of India, the chief of the McCormicks, Andrews and Foxes, was John Morley, the well-known radical author, a "luminary of European learning", a "most honourable man" in the eyes of all European and Russian liberals.

The "European" spirit has already awakened in Asia, the peoples of Asia have become democratic-minded.

Pravda No. 87, April 14, 1913   *Collected Works*, Vol. 19
Signed: W.

THE AWAKENING OF ASIA

Was it so long ago that China was considered typical of the lands that had been standing still for centuries? Today China is a land of seething political activity, the scene of a virile social movement and of a democratic upsurge. Following the 1905 movement in Russia,[26] the democratic revolution spread to the whole of Asia—to Turkey, Persia, China. Ferment is growing in British India.

A significant development is the spread of the revolutionary democratic movement to the Dutch East Indies, to Java and the other Dutch colonies, with a population of some forty million.

First, the democratic movement is developing among the masses of Java, where a nationalist movement has arisen under the banner of Islam. Secondly, capitalism has created a local intelligentsia consisting of acclimatised Europeans who demand independence for the Dutch East Indies. Thirdly, the fairly large Chinese population of Java and the other islands have brought the revolutionary movement from their native land.

Describing this awakening of the Dutch East Indies, van Ravesteyn, a Dutch Marxist, points out that the age-old despotism and tyranny of the Dutch Government now meet with resolute resistance and protest from the masses of the native population.

The usual events of a pre-revolutionary period have begun. Parties and unions are being founded at amazing speed. The government is banning them, thereby only fanning the resentment and accelerating the growth of the movement. Recently, for example, it dissolved the "Indian Party" because its programme and rules spoke of the striving for *independence*. The Dutch *Derzhimordas*[27] (with the approval, incidentally,

22

of the clericals and liberals—European liberalism is rotten to the core!) regarded this clause as a criminal attempt at separation from the Netherlands! The dissolved party was, of course, revived under a different name.

A National Union of the native population has been formed in Java. It already has a membership of 80,000 and is holding mass meetings. There is no stopping the growth of the democratic movement.

World capitalism and the 1905 movement in Russia have finally aroused Asia. Hundreds of millions of the downtrodden and benighted have awakened from medieval stagnation to a new life and are rising to fight for elementary human rights and democracy.

The workers of the advanced countries follow with interest and inspiration this powerful growth of the liberation movement, in all its various forms, in every part of the world. The bourgeoisie of Europe, scared by the might of the working-class movement, is embracing reaction, militarism, clericalism and obscurantism. But the proletariat of the European countries and the young democracy of Asia, fully confident of its strength and with abiding faith in the masses, are advancing to take the place of this decadent and moribund bourgeoisie.

The awakening of Asia and the beginning of the struggle for power by the advanced proletariat of Europe are a symbol of the new phase in world history that began early this century.

Pravda No. 103, May 7, 1913
Signed: *F.*

Collected Works, Vol. 19

THE WORKING CLASS
AND THE NATIONAL QUESTION

Russia is a motley country as far as her nationalities are concerned. Government policy, which is the policy of the landowners supported by the bourgeoisie, is steeped in Black-Hundred nationalism.

This policy is spearheaded against the *majority* of the peoples of Russia who constitute the *majority* of her population. And alongside this we have the bourgeois nationalism of other nations (Polish, Jewish, Ukrainian, Georgian, etc.), raising its head and trying to *divert* the working class from its great world-wide tasks by a national struggle or a struggle for national culture.

The national question must be clearly presented and must be solved by all class-conscious workers.

When the bourgeoisie was fighting for freedom together with the people, together with all those who labour, it stood for full freedom and equal rights for the nations. Advanced countries, Switzerland, Belgium, Norway and others, provide us with an example of how free nations under a really democratic system live together in peace or separate peacefully from each other.

Today the bourgeoisie fears the workers and is seeking an alliance with the Purishkeviches,[28] with the reactionaries, and is betraying democracy, advocating oppression or unequal rights among nations and corrupting the workers with *nationalist* slogans.

In our times the proletariat alone upholds the real freedom of nations and the unity of workers of all nations.

For different nations to live together in peace and freedom or to separate and form different states (if that is more convenient for them), full democracy, upheld by the working class, is essential. No privileges for any nation or any one language! Not even the slightest degree of oppression or the slightest injustice in respect of a national minority—such are the principles of working-class democracy.

The capitalists and landowners want, at all costs, to keep the workers of different nations apart while the powers that be live splendidly together as shareholders in profitable concerns involving millions (such as the Lena Goldfields[29])—Orthodox Christians and Jews, Russians and Germans, Poles and Ukrainians, everyone who possesses *capital*, exploit the workers of all nations in company.

Class-conscious workers stand for *full unity* among the workers of all nations in every educational, trade union, political, etc., workers' organisation. Let the Cadet gentlemen disgrace themselves by denying or belittling the importance of equal rights for Ukrainians. Let the bourgeoisie of all nations find comfort in lying phrases about national culture, national tasks, etc., etc.

The workers will not allow themselves to be disunited by sugary speeches about national culture, or "national-cultural autonomy". The workers of all nations together, concertedly, in organisations common to all, uphold full freedom and complete equality of rights, the guarantee of genuine culture.

The workers of the whole world are building up their own internationalist culture, which the champions of freedom and enemies of oppression have for long been preparing. To the old world, the world of national oppression, national bickering, and national isolation the workers counterpose a new world, a world of the unity of the working people of all nations, a world in which there is no place for any privileges or for the slightest degree of oppression of man by man.

Pravda No. 106, May 10, 1913   *Collected Works*, Vol. 19

BACKWARD EUROPE AND ADVANCED ASIA

The comparison sounds like a paradox. Who does not know that Europe is advanced and Asia backward? But the words taken for this title contain a bitter truth.

In civilised and advanced Europe, with its highly developed machine industry, its rich, multiform culture and its constitutions, a point in history has been reached when the commanding bourgeoisie, fearing the growth and increasing strength of the proletariat, comes out in support of everything backward, moribund and medieval. The bourgeoisie is living out its last days, and is joining with all obsolete and obsolescent forces in an attempt to preserve tottering wage-slavery.

Advanced Europe is commanded by a bourgeoisie which supports everything that is backward. The Europe of our day is advanced not *thanks to*, but *in spite of*, the bourgeoisie, for it is only the proletariat that is adding to the million-strong army of fighters for a better future. It alone preserves and spreads implacable enmity towards backwardness, savagery, privilege, slavery and the humiliation of man by man.

In "advanced" Europe, the *sole advanced* class is the proletariat. As for the living bourgeoisie, it is prepared to go to any length of savagery, brutality and crime in order to uphold dying capitalist slavery.

And a more striking example of this decay of the *entire* European bourgeoisie can scarcely be cited than the support it is lending to *reaction* in Asia in furtherance of the selfish aims of the financial manipulators and capitalist swindlers.

Everywhere in Asia a mighty democratic movement is growing, spreading and gaining in strength. The bourgeoisie there is *as yet* siding with the people against reaction.

Hundreds of millions of people are awakening to life, light and freedom. What delight this world movement is arousing in the hearts of all class-conscious workers, who know that the path to collectivism lies through democracy! What sympathy for young Asia imbues all honest democrats!

And "advanced" Europe? It is plundering China and helping the foes of democracy, the foes of freedom in China!

Here is a simple but instructive little calculation. A new Chinese loan has been concluded *against* Chinese democracy: "Europe" is *for* Yüan Shih-k'ai, who is preparing a military dictatorship. Why does it support him? Because it is good business. The loan has been concluded for about 250,000,000 rubles, at the rate of 84 to a 100. That means that the bourgeois of "Europe" will *pay* the Chinese 210,000,000 rubles, but will take from the public 225,000,000 rubles. There you have at one stroke—a clear profit of *fifteen million rubles* in a few weeks! It really is a *"clear"* profit, isn't it?

What if the Chinese people do not recognise the loan? China, after all, is a republic, and the majority in parliament are *against* the loan.

Oh, then "advanced" Europe will raise a cry about "civilisation", "order", "culture" and "fatherland"! It will set the *guns* in motion and, in alliance with Yüan Shih-k'ai, that adventurer, traitor and friend of reaction, crush a republic in "backward" Asia.

All commanding forces of Europe, all the European bourgeoisie are *in alliance* with all the forces of reaction and medievalism in China.

But all young Asia, that is, the hundreds of millions of Asian working people, has a reliable ally in the proletariat of all civilised countries. No force on earth can prevent the victory of the proletariat, which will liberate both the peoples of Europe and the peoples of Asia.

ON THE NATIONAL PRIDE
OF THE GREAT RUSSIANS

What a lot of talk, argument and vociferation there is nowadays about nationality and the fatherland! Liberal and radical cabinet ministers in Britain, a host of "forward-looking" journalists in France (who have proved in full agreement with their reactionary colleagues), and a swarm of official Cadet* and progressive scribblers in Russia (including several Narodniks[30] and "Marxists")—all have effusive praise for the liberty and the independence of their respective countries, the grandeur of the principle of national independence. Here one cannot tell where the venal eulogist of the butcher Nicholas Romanov or of the brutal oppressors of Negroes and Indians ends, and where the common philistine, who from sheer stupidity or spinelessness drifts with the stream, begins. Nor is that distinction important. We see before us an extensive and very deep ideological trend, whose origins are closely interwoven with the interests of the landowners and the capitalists of the dominant nations. Scores and hundreds of millions are being spent every year for the propaganda of ideas advantageous to those classes: it is a pretty big millrace that takes its waters from all sources—from Menshikov,[31] a chauvinist by conviction, to chauvinists for reason of opportunism or spinelessness, such as Plekhanov and Maslov, Rubanovich and Smirnov, Kropotkin and Burtsev.[32]

Let us, Great-Russian Social-Democrats, also try to define our attitude to this ideological trend. It would be unseemly for us, representatives of a dominant nation in the far east of Europe and a goodly part of Asia, to forget the immense significance of the national question—especially in a country

---

* i.e., liberal-bourgeois—*Ed.*

which has been rightly called the "prison of the peoples", and particularly at a time when, in the far east of Europe and in Asia, capitalism is awakening to life and self-consciousness a number of "new" nations, large and small—at a moment when the tsarist monarchy has called up millions of Great Russians and non-Russians, so as to "solve" a number of national problems in accordance with the interests of the Council of the United Nobility[33] and of the Guchkovs, Krestovnikovs, Dolgorukovs, Kutlers and Rodichevs.[34]

Is a sense of national pride alien to us, Great-Russian class-conscious proletarians? Certainly not! We love our language and our country, and we are doing our very utmost to raise *her* toiling masses (i.e., nine-tenths of *her* population) to the level of a democratic and socialist consciousness. To us it is most painful to see and feel the outrages, the oppression and the humiliation our fair country suffers at the hands of the tsar's butchers, the nobles and the capitalists. We take pride in the resistance to these outrages put up from our midst, from the Great Russians; in *that* midst having produced Radishchev,[35] the Decembrists[36] and the revolutionary commoners of the seventies[37]; in the Great-Russian working class having created, in 1905, a mighty revolutionary party of the masses; and in the Great-Russian peasantry having begun to turn towards democracy and set about overthrowing the clergy and the landed proprietors.

We remember that Chernyshevsky,[38] the Great-Russian democrat, who dedicated his life to the cause of revolution, said half a century ago: "A wretched nation, a nation of slaves, from top to bottom—all slaves.[39]" The overt and covert Great-Russian slaves (slaves with regard to the tsarist monarchy) do not like to recall these words. Yet, in our opinion, these were words of genuine love for our country, a love distressed by the absence of a revolutionary spirit in the masses of the Great-Russian people. There was none of that spirit at the time. There is little of it now, but it already exists. We are full of national pride because the Great-Russian nation, *too,* has created a revolutionary class, because it, *too,* has proved capable of providing mankind with great models of the struggle for freedom and socialism, and not only with great pogroms, rows of gallows, dungeons, great famines and great servility to priests, tsars, landowners and capitalists.

We are full of a sense of national pride, and for that very reason we *particularly* hate *our* slavish past (when the landed nobility led the peasants into war to stifle the freedom of Hungary, Poland, Persia and China), and our slavish present, when these selfsame landed proprietors, aided by the capitalists, are leading us into a war in order to throttle Poland and the Ukraine, crush the democratic movement in Persia and China, and strengthen the gang of Romanovs, Bobrinskys and Purishkeviches,[40] who are a disgrace to our Great-Russian national dignity. Nobody is to be blamed for being born a slave; but a slave who not only eschews a striving for freedom but justifies and eulogises his slavery (e.g., calls the throttling of Poland and the Ukraine, etc., a "defence of the fatherland" of the Great Russians)—such a slave is a lickspittle and a boor, who arouses a legitimate feeling of indignation, contempt, and loathing.

"No nation can be free if it oppresses other nations," said Marx and Engels, the greatest representatives of consistent nineteenth-century democracy, who became the teachers of the revolutionary proletariat. And, full of a sense of national pride, we Great-Russian workers want, come what may, a free and independent, a sovereign, democratic, republican and proud Great Russia, one that will base its relations with its neighbours on the human principle of equality, and not on the feudalist principle of privilege, which is so degrading to a great nation. Just because we want that, we say: it is impossible, in the twentieth century and in Europe (even in the far east of Europe), to "defend the fatherland" otherwise than by using every revolutionary means to combat the monarchy, the landowners and the capitalists of one's *own* fatherland, i.e., the *worst* enemies of our country. We say that the Great Russians cannot "defend the fatherland" otherwise than by desiring the defeat of tsarism in any war, as the lesser evil to nine-tenths of the inhabitants of Great Russia. For tsarism not only oppresses those nine-tenths economically and politically, but also demoralises, degrades, dishonours and prostitutes them by teaching them to oppress other nations and to cover up this shame with hypocritical and quasi-patriotic phrases.

The objection may be advanced that, besides tsarism and under its wing, another historical force has arisen and become strong, viz., Great-Russian capitalism, which is carrying on progressive work by economically centralising and welding together vast regions. This objection, however, does not excuse, but on the contrary still more condemns our socialist-chauvinists, who should be called tsarist-Purishkevich socialists (just as Marx called the Lassalleans Royal-Prussian socialists[41]). Let us even assume that history will decide in favour of Great-Russian dominant-nation capitalism, and against the hundred and one small nations. That is not impossible, for the entire history of capital is one of violence and plunder, blood and corruption. We do not advocate preserving small nations at all costs; *other conditions being equal*, we are decidedly for centralisation and are opposed to the petty-bourgeois ideal of federal relationships. Even if our assumption were true, however, it is, firstly, not our business, that of democrats (let alone of socialists), to help Romanov-Bobrinsky-Purishkevich throttle the Ukraine, etc. In his own Junker[42] fashion, Bismarck accomplished a progressive historical task,[43] but he would be a fine "Marxist" indeed who, on such grounds, thought of justifying socialist support for Bismarck! Moreover, Bismarck promoted economic development by bringing together the disunited Germans, who were being oppressed by other nations. The economic prosperity and rapid development of Great Russia, however, require that the country be liberated from Great-Russian oppression of other nations—that is the difference that our admirers of the true-Russian would-be Bismarcks overlook.

Secondly, if history were to decide in favour of Great-Russian dominant-nation capitalism, it follows hence that the *socialist* role of the Great-Russian proletariat, as the principal driving force of the communist revolution engendered by capitalism, will be all the greater. The proletarian revolution calls for a prolonged education of the workers in the spirit of the *fullest* national equality and brotherhood. Consequently, the interests of the Great-Russian proletariat require that the masses be systematically educated to champion—most resolutely, consistently, boldly and in a revolutionary manner—complete equality and the right to self-determination for all the nations oppressed by the Great Russians. The interests of the Great Russians' national pride (understood, not in the slavish sense) coincide with the *socialist* interests of the

Great-Russian (and all other) proletarians. Our model will always be Marx, who, after living in Britain for decades and becoming half-English, demanded freedom and national independence for Ireland in the interests of the socialist movement of the British workers.

In the second hypothetical case we have considered, our home-grown socialist-chauvinists, Plekhanov, etc., etc., will prove traitors, not only to their own country—a free and democratic Great Russia, but also to the proletarian brotherhood of all the nations of Russia, i.e., to the cause of socialism.

Sotsial-Demokrat No. 35, December 12, 1914

Collected Works, Vol. 21

From
SOCIALISM AND WAR

Chapter I

THE PRINCIPLES OF SOCIALISM
AND THE WAR OF 1914-1915

The Attitude of Socialists Towards Wars

Socialists have always condemned wars between nations as barbarous and brutal. Our attitude towards war, however, is fundamentally different from that of the bourgeois pacifists (supporters and advocates of peace) and of the anarchists. We differ from the former in that we understand the inevitable connection between wars and the class struggle within a country; we understand that wars cannot be abolished unless classes are abolished and socialism is created; we also differ in that we regard civil wars, i.e., wars waged by an oppressed class against the oppressor class, by slaves against slave-holders, by serfs against landowners, and by wage-workers against the bourgeoisie, as fully legitimate, progressive and necessary. We Marxists differ from both pacifists and anarchists in that we deem it necessary to study each war historically (from the standpoint of Marx's dialectical materialism) and separately. There have been in the past numerous wars which, despite all the horrors, atrocities, distress and suffering that inevitably accompany all wars, were progressive, i.e., benefited the development of mankind by helping to destroy most harmful and reactionary institutions (e.g., an autocracy or serfdom) and the most barbarous despotisms in Europe (the Turkish and the Russian). That is why the features historically specific to the present war must come up for examination.

The Historical Types of Wars in Modern Times

The Great French Revolution ushered in a new epoch in the history of mankind. From that time down to the Paris Commune, i.e., between 1789 and 1871, one type of war was of a bourgeois-progressive character, waged for national liberation. In other words, the overthrow of absolutism and feudalism, the undermining of these institutions, and the overthrow of alien oppression, formed the chief content and historical significance of such wars. These were therefore progressive wars; during *such* wars, all honest and revolutionary democrats, as well as all socialists, always wished success to that country (i.e., that bourgeoisie) which had helped to overthrow or undermine the most baneful foundations of feudalism, absolutism and the oppression of other nations. For example, the revolutionary wars[44] waged by France contained an element of plunder and the conquest of foreign territory by the French, but this does not in the least alter the fundamental historical significance of those wars, which destroyed or undermined feudalism and absolutism in the whole of the old, serf-owning Europe. In the Franco-Prussian War,[45] Germany plundered France but this does not alter the fundamental historical significance of that war, which liberated tens of millions of German people from feudal disunity and from the oppression of two despots, the Russian tsar and Napoleon III.

The Difference Between Wars of Aggression and of Defence

The period of 1789-1871 left behind it deep marks and revolutionary memories. There could be no development of the proletarian struggle for socialism prior to the overthrow of feudalism, absolutism and alien oppression. When, in speaking of the wars of *such* periods, socialists stressed the legitimacy of "defensive" wars, they always had these aims in mind, namely revolution against medievalism and serfdom. By a "defensive" war socialists have always understood a "*just*" war in this particular sense (Wilhelm Liebknecht[46] once expressed himself precisely in this way). It is only in this sense that socialists have always regarded wars "for the

34

defence of the fatherland", or "defensive" wars, as legitimate, progressive and just. For example, if tomorrow, Morocco were to declare war on France, or India on Britain, or Persia or China on Russia, and so on, these would be "just", "defensive" wars, *irrespective* of who would be the first to attack; any socialist would wish the oppressed, dependent and unequal states victory over the oppressor, slave-holding and predatory "Great" Powers.

But imagine a slave-holder who owns 100 slaves warring against another who owns 200 slaves, for a more "just" redistribution of slaves. The use of the term of a "defensive" war, or a war "for the defence of the fatherland", would clearly be historically false in such a case and would in practice be sheer deception of the common people, philistines, and the ignorant, by the astute slave-holders. It is in this way that the peoples are being deceived with "national" ideology and the term of "defence of the fatherland" by the present-day imperialist bourgeoisie in the war now being waged between slave-holders with the purpose of consolidating slavery.

The War of Today Is an Imperialist War

It is almost universally admitted that this war is an imperialist war. In most cases, however, this term is distorted, or applied to one side, or else a loophole is left for the assertion that this war may, after all, be bourgeois-progressive, and of significance to the national liberation movement. Imperialism is the highest stage in the development of capitalism, reached only in the twentieth century. Capitalism now finds that the old national states, without whose formation it could not have overthrown feudalism, are too cramped for it. Capitalism has developed concentration to such a degree that entire branches of industry are controlled by syndicates, trusts and associations of capitalist multimillionaires and almost the entire globe has been divided up among the "lords of capital" either in the form of colonies or by entangling other countries in thousands of threads of financial exploitation. Free trade and competition have been superseded by a striving towards monopolies, the seizure of territory for the investment of capital and as sources of raw materials, and so on. From the liberator of nations, which it was in the struggle against feudalism, capitalism in its imperialist stage has turned into the greatest oppressor of nations. Formerly progressive, capitalism has become reactionary; it has developed the forces of production to such a degree that mankind is faced with the alternative of adopting socialism or of experiencing years and even decades of armed struggle between the "Great" Powers for the artificial preservation of capitalism by means of colonies, monopolies, privileges and national oppression of every kind.

A War Between the Biggest Slave-Holders for the Maintenance and Consolidation of Slavery

To make the significance of imperialism clear, we will quote precise figures showing the partition of the world among the so-called "Great" Powers (i.e., those successful in great plunder).

Partition of the World Among the "Great" Slave-holding Powers

"Great" Powers	Colonies				Metropolis		Total	
	1876		1914		1914			
	Square kilo-metres	Population	Square kilo-metres	Population	Square kilo-metres	Population	Square kilo-metres	Population
	millions		millions		millions		millions	
Britain	22.5	251.9	33.5	393.5	0.3	46.5	33.8	440.0
Russia	17.0	15.9	17.4	33.2	5.4	136.2	22.8	169.4
France	0.9	6.0	10.6	55.5	0.5	39.6	11.1	95.1
Germany	—	—	2.9	12.3	0.5	64.9	3.4	77.2
Japan	—	—	0.3	19.2	0.4	53.0	0.7	72.2
United States of America	—	—	0.3	9.7	9.4	97.0	9.7	106.7
Total for the six "Great" Powers	40.4	273.8	65.0	523.4	16.5	437.2	81.5	960.6

"Great" Powers	Colonies				Metropolis		Total	
	1876		1914		1914			
	Square kilometres	Population	Square kilometres	Population	Square kilometres	Population	Square kilometres	Population
	millions		millions		millions		millions	
Colonies belonging to *other* than Great Powers (Belgium, Holland and other states)			9.9	45.3			9.9	45.3
Three "semi-colonial" countries (Turkey, China and Persia) . .							14.5	361.2
Total							105.9	1,367.1
Other states and countries							28.0	289.9
Entire globe (exclusive of Arctic and Antarctic regions) *Grand Total*							133.9	1,657.0

Hence it will be seen that, since 1876, most of the nations which were foremost fighters for freedom in 1789-1871, have, on the basis of a highly developed and "over-mature" capitalism, become oppressors and enslavers of most of the population and the nations of the globe. From 1876 to 1914, six "Great" Powers grabbed 25 million square kilometres, i.e., an area two and a half times that of Europe! Six Powers have enslaved *523 million* people in the colonies. For every four inhabitants in the "Great" Powers there are five in "their" colonies. It is common knowledge that colonies are conquered with fire and sword, that the population of the colonies are brutally treated, and that they are exploited in a thousand ways (by exporting capital, through concessions, etc., cheating in the sale of goods, submission to the authorities of the "ruling" nation, and so on and so forth). The Anglo-French bourgeoisie are deceiving the people when they say that they are waging a war for the freedom of nations and of Belgium; in fact they are waging a war for the purpose of retaining the huge colonies they have grabbed. The German imperialists would free Belgium, etc., at once if the British and French would agree to "fairly" share their colonies with them. A feature of the situation is that in this war the fate of the colonies is being decided by a war on the Continent. From the standpoint of bourgeois justice and national freedom (or the right of nations to existence), Germany might be considered absolutely in the right as against Britain and France, for she has been "done out" of colonies, her enemies are oppressing an immeasurably far larger number of nations than she is, and the Slavs that are being oppressed by her ally, Austria, undoubtedly enjoy far more freedom than those of tsarist Russia, that veritable "prison of nations". Germany, however, is fighting, not for the liberation of nations, but for their oppression. It is not the business of socialists to help the younger and stronger robber (Germany) to plunder the older and overgorged robbers. Socialists must take advantage of the struggle between the robbers to overthrow all of them. To be able to do this, socialists must first of all tell the people the truth, namely, that this war is, in three respects, a war between slave-holders with the aim of consolidating slavery. This is a war, firstly, to increase the enslavement of the colonies by means of a "more equitable" distribution and subsequent "more concerted" exploitation of them; secondly, to increase the oppression of other nations within the "Great" Powers, since *both* Austria and Russia (Russia in greater degree and with results far worse than Austria) maintain their rule only by such oppression, intensifying it by means of war; and thirdly, to increase and prolong wage slavery, since the proletariat is split up and suppressed, while the capitalists are the gainers, making fortunes out of the war, fanning national prejudices and intensifying reaction, which has raised its head in all countries, even in the freest and most republican.

"War Is the Continuation of Politics
by Other" (i.e.: Violent) "Means"

This famous dictum was uttered by Clausewitz, one of the profoundest writers on the problems of war. Marxists have always rightly regarded this thesis as the theoretical basis of views on the significance of any war. It was from this viewpoint that Marx and Engels always regarded the various wars.

Apply this view to the present war. You will see that for decades, for almost half a century, the governments and the ruling classes of Britain and France, Germany and Italy, Austria and Russia have pursued a policy of plundering colonies, oppressing other nations, and suppressing the working-class movement. It is this, and only this, policy that is being continued in the present war. In particular, the policy of both Austria and Russia, in peacetime as well as in wartime, is a policy of enslaving nations, not of liberating them. In China, Persia, India and other dependent countries, on the contrary, we have seen during the past decades a policy of rousing tens and hundreds of millions of people to a national life, of their liberation from the reactionary "Great" Powers' oppression. A war waged on such a historical basis can even today be a bourgeois-progressive war of national liberation.

If the present war is regarded as a continuation of the politics of the "Great" Powers and of the principal classes within them, a glance will immediately reveal the glaring anti-historicity, falseness and hypocrisy of the view that the "defence-of-the-fatherland" idea can be justified in the present war.

The Case of Belgium

The favourite plea of the social-chauvinists of the Triple (now Quadruple) Entente[47] (in Russia, Plekhanov and Co.) is the case of Belgium. This instance, however, speaks against them. The German imperialists have brazenly violated the neutrality of Belgium, as belligerent states have done always and everywhere, trampling upon *all* treaties and obligations if necessary. Let us suppose that all states interested in the observance of international treaties should declare war on Germany with the demand that Belgium be liberated and indemnified. In that case, the sympathies of socialists would, of course, be with Germany's enemies. But the whole point is that the Triple (and Quadruple) Entente is waging war *not* over Belgium; this is common knowledge and only hypocrites disguise the fact. Britain is grabbing at Germany's colonies and Turkey; Russia is grabbing at Galicia and Turkey, France wants Alsace-Lorraine and even the left bank of the Rhine; a treaty has been concluded with Italy for the division of the spoils (Albania and Asia Minor); bargaining is going on with Bulgaria and Rumania, also for the division of the spoils. In the present war waged by the governments of today, it is *impossible* to help Belgium *otherwise* than by helping to throttle Austria or Turkey, etc.! Where does "defence of the fatherland" come in here? Herein lies the specific feature of imperialist war, a war between reactionary-bourgeois and historically outmoded governments, waged for the purpose of oppressing other nations. Whoever justifies participation in the present war is perpetuating the imperialist oppression of nations. Whoever advocates taking advantage of the present embarrassments of the governments so as to fight for the social revolution is championing the real freedom of really all nations, which is possible only under socialism.

Written between July and August 1915

Published late in 1915 as a separate pamphlet by *Sotsial-Demokrat* editors in Geneva

Collected Works, Vol. 21

From
A CARICATURE OF MARXISM
AND IMPERIALIST ECONOMISM

6. THE OTHER POLITICAL ISSUES RAISED
AND DISTORTED BY P. KIEVSKY

Liberation of the colonies, we stated in our theses, means self-determination of nations. Europeans often forget that colonial peoples *too* are nations, but to tolerate this "forgetfulness" is to tolerate chauvinism.

P. Kievsky "objects":

In the pure type of colonies, "there is *no* proletariat in the proper sense of the term" (end of §r, Chapter II). "For whom, then, is the 'self-determination' slogan meant? For the colonial bourgeoisie? For the fellahs? For the peasants? Certainly not. It is absurd for *socialists* [Kievsky's italics] to demand self-determination for the colonies, for it is absurd in general to advance the slogans of a workers' party for countries where there are no workers."

P. Kievsky's anger and his denunciation of our view as "absurd" notwithstanding, we make bold to submit that his arguments are erroneous. Only the late and unlamented Economists[48] believed that the "slogans of a workers' party" are issued *only* for workers.* No, these slogans are issued for the whole of the labouring population, for the entire people. The democratic part of our programme—Kievsky has given no thought to its significance "in general"—is addressed specifically to the whole people and that is why in it we speak of the "people".**

---

* P. Kievsky would do well to reread what A. Martynov and Co. wrote in 1899-1901. He would find many of his "own" arguments there.

** Some curious opponents of "self-determination of nations" try to refute our views with the argument that "nations" are divided into classes! Our customary reply to these caricature Marxists is that the democratic part of our programme speaks of "government by the people".

The colonial and semi-colonial nations, we said, account for 1,000 million people, and P. Kievsky has not taken the trouble to refute that concrete statement. Of these 1,000 million, more than 700 million (China, India, Persia, Egypt) live in countries where *there are* workers. But even with regard to colonial countries where there are no workers, only slave-owners and slaves, etc., the demand for "self-determination", far from being *absurd*, is *obligatory* for every Marxist. And if he gave the matter a little thought, Kievsky would probably realise this, and also that "self-determination" is always advanced "for" *two* nations: the oppressed and the oppressing.

Another of Kievsky's "objections":

"For that reason we limit ourselves, in respect to the colonies, to a negative slogan, i.e., to the demand socialists present to their governments—'get out of the colonies!' Unachievable within the framework of capitalism, this demand serves to intensify the struggle against imperialism, but does not contradict the trend of development, for a socialist society will not possess colonies."

The author's inability, or reluctance, to give the slightest thought to the theoretical contents of political slogans is simply amazing! Are we to believe that the use of a propaganda phrase instead of a theoretically precise political term alters matters? To say "get out of the colonies" is to evade a theoretical analysis and hide behind propaganda phrases! For every one of our Party propagandists, in referring to the Ukraine, Poland, Finland, etc., is fully entitled to demand of the tsarist government (his "own government"): "get out of Finland", etc. However, the intelligent propagandist will understand that we must not advance either positive or negative slogans for the sole purpose of "intensifying" the struggle. Only men of the Alexinsky[49] type could insist that the "negative" slogan "get out of the Black-Hundred Duma" was justified by the desire to "intensify" the struggle against a certain evil.

Intensification of the struggle is an empty phrase of the subjectivists, who forget the Marxist requirement that every slogan be justified by a precise analysis of *economic* realities, the *political* situation and the *political* significance of the slogan. It is embarrassing to have to drive this home, but what can one do?

We know the Alexinsky habit of cutting short a theoretical discussion of a theoretical question by propaganda outcries. It is a bad habit. The slogan "get out of the colonies" has one and only one political and economic content: freedom of secession for the colonial nations, freedom to establish a separate state! If, as P. Kievsky believes, the *general* laws of imperialism prevent the self-determination of nations and make it a utopia, illusion, etc., etc., then how can one, without stopping to think, make an exception from these general laws for *most* of the nations of the world? Obviously, P. Kievsky's "theory" is a caricature of theory.

Commodity production and capitalism, and the connecting threads of finance capital, exist in the vast majority of colonial countries. How, then, can we urge the imperialist countries, their governments, to "get out of the colonies" if, *from the standpoint* of commodity production, capitalism and imperialism, this is an "unscientific" and "utopian" demand, "refuted" *even* by Lensch, Cunow[50] and the rest?

There is not even a shadow of *thought* in the author's argumentation!

He has given no thought to the fact that liberation of the colonies is "unrealisable" *only* in the sense of being "unrealisable without a series of revolutions". He has given no thought to the fact that it is realisable *in conjunction* with a socialist revolution in Europe. He has given no thought to the fact that a "socialist society will not possess" *not only* colonies, but subject nations *in general*. He has given no thought to the fact that, on the question under discussion, there is *no* economic or political difference between Russia's "possession" of Poland or Turkestan. He has given no thought to the fact that a "socialist society" will wish to "get out of the colonies" *only* in the sense of granting them the free *right* to secede, but definitely *not in the sense of* recommending secession.

And for this differentiation between the right to secede and the recommendation to secede, P. Kievsky condemns us as "jugglers", and to "scientifically substantiate" that verdict in the eyes of the workers, he writes:

43

"What is a worker to think when he asks a propagandist how the proletariat should regard *samostiinost* [political independence for the Ukraine], and gets this answer: socialists are working for the right to secede, but their propaganda is against secession?"

I believe I can give a fairly accurate reply to that question, namely: every sensible worker will *think* that Kievsky is *not capable of thinking.*

Every sensible worker will "think": here we have P. Kievsky telling us workers to shout "get out of the colonies". In other words, we Great-Russian workers must demand from our government that it get out of Mongolia, Turkestan, Persia; English workers must demand that the English Government get out of Egypt, India, Persia, etc. But does this mean that *we* proletarians *wish* to separate ourselves from the Egyptian workers and fellahs, from the Mongolian, Turkestan or Indian workers and peasants? Does it mean that *we* advise the labouring masses of the colonies to "separate" from the class-conscious European proletariat? Nothing of the kind. Now, as always, we stand and shall continue to stand for the closest association and merging of the class-conscious workers of the advanced countries with the workers, peasants and slaves of *all* the oppressed countries. We have always advised and shall continue to advise all the oppressed classes in all the oppressed countries, the colonies included, *not* to separate from us, but to form the closest possible ties and merge with us.

We demand from our governments that they quit the colonies, or, to put it in precise political terms rather than in agitational outcries—that they *grant* the colonies full *freedom* of secession, the genuine *right to self-determination,* and we ourselves are sure to implement this right, and grant this freedom, as soon as we capture power. We demand this from existing governments, and will *do* this when we are the government, *not* in order to "recommend" secession, but, on the contrary, in order to facilitate and accelerate the *democratic* association and merging of nations. We shall exert every effort to foster association and merger with the Mongolians, Persians, Indians, Egyptians. We believe it is our duty and *in our interest* to do this, for otherwise socialism in Europe will *not be secure.* We shall endeavour to render these nations, more backward and oppressed than we are, "disinterested cultural assistance", to borrow the happy expression of the Polish Social-Democrats. In other words, we will help them pass to the use of machinery, to the lightening of labour, to democracy, to socialism.

We demand freedom of secession for the Mongolians, Persians, Egyptians and *all* other oppressed and unequal nations without exception, not because *we favour secession,* but *only* because we stand for *free, voluntary* association and merging as distinct from forcible association. That is the *only* reason!

And in this respect the *only* difference between the Mongolian or Egyptian peasants and workers and their Polish or Finnish counterparts is, in our view, that the latter are more developed, more experienced politically than the Great Russians, more economically prepared, etc., and for that reason will in all likelihood *very soon* convince their peoples that it is unwise to extend their present legitimate hatred of the Great Russians, for their role of hangman, to the *socialist* workers and to a socialist Russia. They will convince them that economic expediency and internationalist and democratic instinct and consciousness demand the earliest association of all nations and their merging in a socialist society. And since the Poles and Finns are highly cultured people, they will, in all probability, very soon come to see the correctness of this attitude, and the possible secession of Poland and Finland after the triumph of socialism will therefore be only of short duration. The incomparably less cultured fellahs, Mongolians and Persians might secede for a longer period, but we shall try to shorten it by disinterested cultural assistance as indicated above.

There is *no* other difference in our attitude to the Poles and Mongolians, nor can there be. There is *no* "contradiction", nor can there be, between our propaganda of freedom of secession and our firm resolve to implement that freedom when *we* are the government, and our propaganda of association and merging of nations. That is what, we feel sure, every sensible worker, every genuine socialist and internationalist will "think" of our controversy with P. Kievsky.*

---

* Evidently Kievsky simply *repeated* the slogan "get out of the

Running through the article is Kievsky's basic doubt: why advocate and, when we are in power, implement the freedom of nations to *secede*, considering that the trend of development is towards the *merging* of nations? For the same reason —we reply—that we advocate and, when in power, will implement the dictatorship of the proletariat, though the entire trend of development is towards abolition of coercive domination of one part of society over another. Dictatorship is domination of one part of society over the rest of society, and domination, moreover, that rests directly on coercion. Dictatorship of the proletariat, the only consistently revolutionary class, is necessary to overthrow the bourgeoisie and repel its attempts at counter-revolution. The question of proletarian dictatorship is of such overriding importance that he who denies the need for such dictatorship, or recognises it only in words, cannot be a member of the Social-Democratic Party. However, it cannot be denied that in individual cases, by way of exception, for instance, in some small country after the social revolution has been accomplished in a neighbouring big country, peaceful surrender of power by the bourgeoisie is *possible*, if it is convinced that resistance is hopeless and if it prefers to save its skin. It is much more likely, of course, that even in small states socialism will *not* be achieved without civil war, and for that reason the *only* programme of international Social-Democracy must be recognition of civil war, though violence is, of course, alien to our ideals. The same,

---

colonies", advanced by certain German and Dutch Marxists, without considering not only its theoretical content and implications, but also the specific features of Russia. It is pardonable—to a certain extent— for a Dutch or German Marxist to confine himself to the slogan "get out of the colonies". For, first, the *typical* form of national oppression, in the case of most West European countries, is oppression of the colonies, and, second, the very term "colony" has an especially clear, graphic and vital meaning for West European countries.

But what of Russia? Its peculiarity lies precisely in the fact that the difference between *"our"* "colonies" and "our" oppressed nations is not clear, not concrete and not vitally felt!

For a Marxist writing in, say, German it might be pardonable to overlook *this* peculiarity of Russia; for Kievsky it is unpardonable. The sheer absurdity of trying to discover some serious difference between oppressed nations and colonies in the case of Russia should be especially clear to a Russian socialist who wants not simply to *repeat*, but to *think*.

mutatis mutandis (with the *necessary* alterations), is applicable to nations. We favour their merger, but *now* there can be no transition from forcible merger, from annexation, to voluntary merger without freedom of secession. We recognise –and quite rightly–the predominance of the economic factor, but to interpret it *à la* Kievsky is to make a caricature of Marxism. Even the trusts and banks of modern imperialism, though inevitable everywhere as part of developed capitalism, differ in their concrete aspects from country to country. There is a still greater difference, despite homogeneity in essentials, between political forms in the advanced imperialist countries–America, England, France, Germany. The same variety will manifest itself also in the path mankind will follow from the imperialism of today to the socialist revolution of tomorrow. All nations will arrive at socialism–this is inevitable, but all will do so in not exactly the same way, each will contribute something of its own to some form of democracy, to some variety of the dictatorship of the proletariat, to the varying rate of socialist transformations in the different aspects of social life. There is nothing more primitive from the viewpoint of theory, or more ridiculous from that of practice, than to paint, "in the name of historical materialism", *this* aspect of the future in a monotonous grey. The result will be nothing more than Suzdal daubing.[51] And even if reality were to show that *prior* to the first victory of the socialist proletariat only 1/500 of the nations now oppressed will win emancipation and secede, that *prior* to the final victory of the socialist proletariat the world over (i.e., during all the vicissitudes of the socialist revolution) also only 1/500 of the oppressed nations will secede for a very short time–*even* in that event we would be correct, both from the theoretical and practical political standpoint, in advising the workers, already now, not to permit into their Social-Democratic parties those socialists of the oppressor nations who do not recognise and do not advocate freedom of secession for *all* oppressed nations. For the fact is that we do not know, and cannot know, how many of the oppressed nations will in practice require secession in order to contribute something of their own to the different *forms* of democracy, the different *forms* of transition to socialism. And that the negation of freedom of secession now is theoretically false from beginning to end and in practice amounts to servility to the chauvinists of the oppressing nations—this we know, see and feel daily.

Written August-October 1916

First published in the magazine
Zvezda Nos. 1 and 2, 1924

Signed: *V. Lenin*

Collected Works, Vol. 23

From

REPLIES TO QUESTIONS PUT
BY KARL WIEGAND,
BERLIN CORRESPONDENT OF
UNIVERSAL SERVICE

2. What are our plans in Asia?

They are the same as in Europe: peaceful coexistence with all peoples; with the workers and peasants of all nations awakening to a new life—a life without exploiters, without landowners, without capitalists, without merchants. The imperialist war of 1914-18, the war of the capitalists of the Anglo-French (and Russian) group against the German-Austrian capitalist group for the partition of the world, has awakened Asia and has strengthened there, as everywhere else, the urge towards freedom, towards peaceful labour and against possible future wars.

February 18, 1920

Published on February 23, 1920
in the *Daily Express* No. 6198

Collected Works, Vol. 30

First published in Russian in
Pravda No. 112, April 22, 1950

TO THE INDIAN REVOLUTIONARY ASSOCIATION[52]

I am glad to hear that the principles of self-determination and liberation of oppressed nations from exploitation by foreign and native capitalists, proclaimed by the Workers' and Peasants' Republic, have found such a ready response among progressive Indians, who are waging a heroic fight for freedom. The toiling masses of Russia follow the awakening of the Indian worker and peasant with unabating attention. The organisation and discipline of the working people and their perseverance and solidarity with the workers of the world are an earnest of ultimate success. We welcome the close alliance of Moslem and non-Moslem elements. We sincerely want to see this alliance extended to all the toilers of the East. For only when the Indian, Chinese, Korean, Japanese, Persian, Turkish workers and peasants join hands and march together in the common cause of liberation—only then will decisive victory over the exploiters be ensured. Long live free Asia!

Pravda No. 108, and *Izvestia* No. 108, May 20, 1920

Collected Works, Vol. 31

REPORT OF THE COMMISSION
ON THE NATIONAL AND COLONIAL QUESTIONS
TO THE SECOND CONGRESS
OF THE COMMUNIST INTERNATIONAL

July 26, 1920

Comrades, I shall confine myself to a brief introduction, after which Comrade Maring, who was secretary of our commission, will give you a detailed account of the changes we have made in the theses. He will be followed by Comrade Roy[53] who formulated supplementary theses. Our commission unanimously adopted both the preliminary theses, as amended, and the supplementary theses. We have thus reached complete unanimity on all major issues. I shall now make a few brief remarks.

First, what is the cardinal, underlying idea of our theses? The distinction between oppressed and oppressor nations. And unlike the Second International[54] and bourgeois democracy, we emphasise this distinction. In this age of imperialism, it is particularly important for the proletariat and the Communist International to establish concrete economic facts and to proceed from concrete realities and not from abstract postulates in the solution of all colonial and national problems.

The characteristic feature of imperialism is the division of the whole world, as we now see, into a large number of oppressed nations and an insignificant number of oppressor nations which, however, command colossal wealth and powerful armed forces. The overwhelming majority of the world's population, more than a thousand million, very probably even 1,250 million people—if we take the total population of the world as 1,750 million—or about seventy per cent of the world's population, is accounted for by oppressed nations, which are either in a state of direct colonial dependence or represent semi-colonies, as, for example, Persia, Turkey and China, or, having suffered defeat at the hands of a big imperialist power, have been made greatly dependent on that power by virtue of peace treaties. This distinction, this idea of dividing the nations into oppressor and oppressed, runs through all the theses, not only the first theses published earlier over my signature, but also the theses presented by Comrade Roy. The latter were framed chiefly from the standpoint of the situation in India and other big Asian countries oppressed by Britain. That is what makes them so valuable.

The second basic idea of our theses is that in the present world situation, after the imperialist war, international relations, the whole world system of states, are determined by the struggle of a small group of imperialist nations against the Soviet movement and the Soviet states headed by Soviet Russia. Unless we bear that in mind, we shall not be able to present a single national and colonial question correctly, even if it concerns a very remote part of the world. The Communist parties, both in civilised and backward countries alike, can present and settle political questions correctly only if they make this their starting point.

Thirdly, I should like especially to emphasise the question of the bourgeois-democratic movement in backward countries. It was this question that gave rise to some differences. We discussed whether it would be correct, in principle and in theory, to state that the Communist International and the Communist parties must support the bourgeois-democratic movement in backward countries. As a result of our discussion, we arrived at the unanimous decision to speak of the national-revolutionary movement rather than the "bourgeois-democratic" movement. There need not be the slightest doubt that every national movement can only be a bourgeois-democratic movement, for the overwhelming mass of the population in backward countries consists of peasants who represent bourgeois-capitalist relationships. It would be utopian to believe that proletarian parties, if indeed they can emerge in these backward countries, could pursue communist tactics and a communist policy without establishing definite relations with the peasant movement and without giving it effective support. But it was objected that if we speak of the bourgeois-democratic movement, we shall be obliterating all distinction between the reformist and the revolutionary movement. Yet that distinction has been very clearly revealed of late in backward and colonial countries, for the imperialist bourgeoisie is doing everything within its power to implant a reformist movement among the oppressed nations too. There has been a certain *rapprochement* between the bourgeoisie of the exploiting countries and those of the colonial countries, so that very often—perhaps even in most cases— although the bourgeoisie of the oppressed countries does support the national movement, it is working hand in glove with the imperialist bourgeoisie, that is, joins forces with it against all revolutionary movements and revolutionary classes. This was irrefutably demonstrated in the commission, and we decided that the only correct thing was to take this distinction into account and in nearly all cases substitute the term "national-revolutionary" for the term "bourgeois-democratic". The significance of this change is that we, as Communists, should, and will, support bourgeois liberation movements in the colonies only when they are genuinely revolutionary, and when their exponents do not hinder our work of educating and organising the peasantry and the broad mass of the exploited in a revolutionary spirit. If these conditions do not exist, the Communists in these countries must combat the reformist bourgeoisie, among which are also the heroes of the Second International. Reformist parties already exist in the colonial countries, and in some cases their spokesmen call themselves Social-Democrats and socialists. The distinction I referred to has been made in all the theses with the result, I think, that our view is now formulated much more precisely.

Next, I would like to make a remark on peasants' Soviets. The practical activities of the Russian Communists in the former tsarist colonies, in such backward countries as Turkestan, etc., confronted us with the question of how to apply the communist tactics and policy in pre-capitalist conditions. For the chief determining feature in these countries is the domination of pre-capitalist relationships, and there can therefore be no question of a purely proletarian movement. There is practically no industrial proletariat in these countries.

Despite this, however, even there we have assumed, we must assume, the role of leader. Experience showed that we have to overcome colossal difficulties in these countries. But the practical results achieved are proof that despite these difficulties we are in a position to inspire in the masses the urge for independent political thought and independent political action even where there is practically no proletariat. For us this work is more difficult than it will be for comrades in the West European countries, because in Russia the proletariat is overwhelmed with the work of state administration. And it is quite understandable that peasants living in semi-feudal dependence can fully appreciate the idea of Soviet organisation and translate it into practice. It is also clear that the oppressed masses, those who are exploited not only by merchant capital but also by the feudals, and by a state based on feudalism, can apply this weapon, this type of organisation in their own conditions too. The idea of Soviet organisation is a simple one, and is applicable not only to proletarian, but also to peasant feudal and semi-feudal relations. Our experience in this respect is not very considerable as yet, but the debate in the commission, in which several representatives from colonial countries participated, convincingly demonstrated that the Communist International theses should indicate that peasants' Soviets, Soviets of the exploited, are a weapon that can be employed not only in capitalist countries, but also in countries with pre-capitalist relations, and it is the bounden duty of Communist parties, and of the elements that are prepared to found Communist parties, to conduct propaganda in favour of peasants' Soviets, or working people's Soviets, everywhere, backward countries and colonies included. Wherever conditions permit, they must make immediate attempts to set up Soviets of the working people.

This opens up a very interesting and very important field for practical activity. So far our common experience in this respect is not very great, but gradually more and more data will accumulate. There can be no question but that the proletariat of the advanced countries can and should assist the labouring masses of the backward countries and that the backward countries can develop and emerge from their present state when the victorious proletariat of the Soviet

Republics extends a helping hand to these masses and is in a position to give them support.

There was a rather lively debate on this question in the commission, and not only in connection with my theses, but still more in connection with Comrade Roy's theses, which he will defend here and certain amendments to which were adopted unanimously.

This is how the question had been presented. Is it true that the capitalist stage of economic development is inevitable for those backward nations which are now liberating themselves and in which some progress is to be observed since the war? We replied in the negative. If the victorious revolutionary proletariat conducts systematic propaganda among them, while the Soviet governments come to their assistance with all the means at their command—in that event, it would be wrong to assume that the capitalist stage of development is inevitable for the backward nationalities. In all the colonies and backward countries, we should not only build independent contingents of fighters and party organisations; not only launch immediate propaganda for the organisation of peasants' Soviets and strive to adapt them to pre-capitalist conditions, but the Communist International should advance and theoretically substantiate the proposition that these backward countries can, with the aid of the proletariat of the advanced countries, go over to the Soviet system and, through definite stages of development, to communism, without having to pass through the capitalist stage.

The necessary means for this cannot be indicated beforehand. Practical experience will suggest them. But it has been definitely established that the idea of Soviets is understood by the mass of working people of even the most remote nations, that the Soviets should be adapted to the conditions of the pre-capitalist social system, and that the Communist parties should immediately, and in all parts of the world, begin work in this direction.

I wish also to mention the importance of revolutionary work by the Communist parties not only in their own countries, but also in colonial countries, and particularly among the troops which the exploiting nations employ to keep the colonial peoples in subjection.

Comrade Quelch of the British Socialist Party spoke of this

in our commission. He said that the rank-and-file English worker would consider it treachery to help the enslaved nations in their revolts against British rule. True, the jingoist and chauvinist-minded labour aristocrats of Britain and America represent a very great danger for socialism, and a very strong pillar of the Second International. We are here confronted with the greatest treachery by the leaders and workers belonging to this bourgeois International. The colonial question was discussed in the Second International too. The Basle Manifesto[55] is quite clear on this point, too. The parties of the Second International pledged revolutionary action, but they have given no sign of genuine revolutionary work or of assistance to the exploited and dependent nations in their revolt against the oppressor nations. And this, I think, applies also to most of the parties that have withdrawn from the Second International and wish to join the Third International. This we must declare publicly, for all to hear, and this cannot be refuted. We shall see if any attempt is made to refute it.

All these considerations were made the basis of our resolutions which undoubtedly are too long, but which, I feel sure, will nevertheless prove of value and will assist in the development and organisation of genuine revolutionary work in connection with the colonial and national questions. And that is our principal task.

First published in full in 1921 in *The Second Congress of the Communist International Verbatim Report*

Collected Works, Vol. 31

ON THE TENTH ANNIVERSARY OF *PRAVDA*

It is ten years since the founding of *Pravda*,[56] the legal—legal under *tsarist* law—Bolshevik daily paper. This decade was preceded by, approximately, another decade: nine years (1903-12) since the emergence of Bolshevism, or thirteen years (1900-12), if we count from the founding in 1900 of the "Bolshevik-oriented" old *Iskra*.[57]

Ten years of publication in Russia of a daily Bolshevik paper.... Only ten years! But measured in terms of our struggle and movement they are equal to a hundred years. For the pace of social development in the past five years has been positively staggering if we apply the old yardstick of the European philistines, the heroes of the Second and Two-and-a-Half Internationals.[58] These civilised philistines are accustomed to regard as "natural" a situation in which hundreds of millions of people (over a billion, to be exact) in the colonies and semi-dependent and appallingly poor countries tolerate the treatment meted out to the Indians and Chinese. They tolerate incredible exploitation, and outright depredation, and hunger, and violence, and humiliation, all in order that "civilised" men might "freely", "democratically", according to "parliamentary procedure", decide whether the booty should be divided up peacefully, or whether a dozen million or so must be done to death in this division of the imperialist booty, yesterday between Germany and Britain, tomorrow between Japan and America (with France and Britain participating in one form or another).

The basic reason for this tremendous acceleration of world development is that new hundreds of millions have been drawn into it. The old bourgeois and imperialist Europe, which was accustomed to look upon itself as the centre of the universe, rotted and burst like a putrid ulcer in the first imperialist holocaust. No matter how the Spenglers,[59] and all the enlightened philistines who are capable of admiring (or even studying) Spengler may lament it, this decline of the old Europe is but an episode in the history of the downfall of the world bourgeoisie, oversatiated by imperialist rapine and oppression of the majority of the world's population.

That majority has now awakened and has begun a movement which even the "mightiest" powers cannot stem. They stand no chance. For the present "victors" in the first imperialist slaughter have not even the strength to score victory over small–tiny, I might say–Ireland, nor can they emerge victorious from the financial confusion that reigns in their own midst. Meanwhile, India and China are seething. They represent over 700 million people, and together with the neighbouring Asian countries, that are in all ways similar to them, over half of the world's inhabitants. Inexorably and with mounting momentum they are approaching their 1905, with the essential and important difference that in 1905 the revolution in Russia could still proceed (at any rate at the beginning) in isolation, that is, without other countries being immediately drawn in. But the revolutions that are maturing in India and China are being drawn into–have already been drawn into–the revolutionary struggle, the revolutionary movement, the world revolution.

The tenth anniversary of *Pravda*, the legal Bolshevik daily, is a graphic illustration of one aspect of this acceleration of the greatest world revolution. In 1906-07, it seemed that the tsarist government has utterly crushed the revolution. A few years later the Bolshevik Party was able–*in a different form, by a different method*–to penetrate into the very citadel of the enemy and daily, "legally", proceed with its work of undermining the accursed tsarist and landowner autocracy from within. A few more years passed, and the proletarian revolution, organised by Bolshevism, triumphed.

Only half a score of revolutionaries shared in the founding of the old *Iskra* in 1900, and only two score or so attended the birth of Bolshevism at the illegal congresses in Brussels and London in 1903.[60]

In 1912-13, when the legal Bolshevik *Pravda* came into being, it had the support of hundreds of thousands of workers who made modest contributions[61] and were able to overcome both the oppression of tsarism and the competition of the Mensheviks, those petty-bourgeois betrayers of socialism.

In November 1917, nine million electors out of a total of thirty-six million voted for the Bolsheviks in the elections to the Constituent Assembly. But if we take the actual struggle, and not merely the elections, at the close of October and in November 1917, the Bolsheviks had the support of the *majority* of the proletariat and class-conscious peasantry, as represented by the majority of the delegates at the Second All-Russia Congress of Soviets,[62] and by the majority of the most active and politically conscious section of the people, namely, the twelve-million army.

These few figures illustrating the "acceleration" of the world revolutionary movement in the past twenty years provide a small and very incomplete picture. They afford only a very approximate idea of the history of no more than 150 million people, whereas in these twenty years the revolution has begun and developed into an invincible force in countries with a total population of over one billion (the whole of Asia, not to forget South Africa, which recently reminded the world of its claim to *human* and not slavish existence, and by methods which were not altogether "parliamentary"[63]).

Some Spenglerite freaks—I apologise for the expression—may conclude (every variety of nonsense can be expected from the "clever" leaders of the Second and Two-and-a-Half Internationals) that this estimate of the revolutionary forces fails to take into account the European and American proletariat. These "clever" leaders always argue as if the fact that birth comes nine months after conception necessarily means that it is possible to define the exact hour and minute of birth as well as the position of the infant during delivery, the condition of the mother and the exact degree of pain and danger both will suffer. Very "clever"! They cannot for the life of them understand that, from the point of view of the development of the international revolution, the transition from Chartism[64] to the servility of a Henderson,[65] or the transition from Varlin to Renaudel,[66] from Wilhelm Liebknecht and Bebel to Südekum, Scheidemann and Noske,[67] can only be likened to an automobile passing *from* a smooth highway stretching for hundreds of miles *to* a dirty stinking puddle on that highway stretching for a few yards.

Men are the makers of history. But the Chartists, the Varlins and the Liebknechts applied their minds and hearts to the making of history. The leaders of the Second and Two-and-a-Half Internationals apply another part of the anatomy: they fertilise the ground for the appearance of new Chartists, new Varlins and new Liebknechts.

At this *most difficult* moment, it would be most harmful for revolutionaries to indulge in self-deception. Though Bolshevism *has become* an international force, though in *all* the civilised and advanced countries new Chartists, new Varlins, new Liebknechts have come to the fore, and are growing in the shape of legal (just as legal as our *Pravda* was under the tsars ten years ago) Communist parties, nonetheless, for the time being, the international bourgeoisie still remains incomparably stronger than its class enemy. This bourgeoisie, which has done everything in its power to hamper the birth of proletarian power in Russia and to multiply tenfold the dangers and suffering attending its birth, is still in a position to condemn millions and tens of millions to torment and death through its whiteguard and imperialist wars, etc. That we must not forget. And we must skilfully adapt our tactics to this peculiar situation. The bourgeoisie is still able freely to torment, torture and kill. But it cannot halt the inevitable and—from the standpoint of world history—rapidly approaching complete triumph of the revolutionary proletariat.

Written on May 2, 1922   *Collected Works*, Vol. 33

Published in *Pravda* No. 98,
May 5, 1922

Signed: *N. Lenin*

Continuation of the notes.
December 30, 1922

THE QUESTION OF NATIONALITIES
OR "AUTONOMISATION"

I suppose I have been very remiss with respect to the workers of Russia for not having intervened energetically and decisively enough in the notorious question of autonomisation,[68] which, it appears, is officially called the question of the Union of Soviet Socialist Republics.

When this question arose last summer, I was ill; and then in autumn I relied too much on my recovery and on the October and December plenary meetings giving me an opportunity of intervening in this question. However, I did not manage to attend the October Plenary Meeting (when this question came up) or the one in December, and so the question passed me by almost completely.

I have only had time for a talk with Comrade Dzerzhinsky, who came from the Caucasus and told me how this matter stood in Georgia. I also managed to exchange a few words with Comrade Zinoviev and express my apprehensions on this matter. From what I was told by Comrade Dzerzhinsky, who was at the head of the commission sent by the C.C. to "investigate" the Georgian incident,[69] I could only draw the greatest apprehensions. If matters had come to such a pass that Orjonikidze could go to the extreme of applying physical violence, as Comrade Dzerzhinsky informed me, we can imagine what a mire we got ourselves into. Obviously the whole business of "autonomisation" was radically wrong and badly timed.

It is said that a united apparatus was needed. Where did that assurance come from? Did it not come from that same Russian apparatus which, as I pointed out in one of the preceding sections of my diary, we took over from tsarism and painted a little with the Soviet brush?

There is no doubt that that measure should have been delayed somewhat until we could say that we vouched for our apparatus as our own. But now we must, in all conscience, admit the contrary; the apparatus we call ours is, in fact, still quite alien to us; it is a bourgeois and tsarist hotch-potch and there has been no possibility of getting rid of it in the course of the past five years without the help of other countries and because we have been "busy" most of the time with military engagements and the fight against famine.

It is quite natural that in such circumstances the "freedom to withdraw from the union" by which we justify ourselves will be a mere scrap of paper, unable to defend the non-Russians from the onslaught of that really Russian man, the Great-Russian chauvinist, in substance a rascal and lover of violence, such as the typical Russian bureaucrat is. There is no doubt that the infinitesimal percentage of Soviet and sovietised workers will drown in that sea of chauvinistic Great-Russian riff-raff like a fly in milk.

It is said in defence of this measure that the People's Commissariats directly concerned with national psychology and national education were set up as separate bodies. But there the question arises: can these People's Commissariats be made quite independent? and, secondly: were we careful enough to take measures that would give the people of other nationalities a real defence against the genuine Russian Derzhimordas? I do not think we took such measures although we could and should have done so.

I think that Stalin's haste and his infatuation with pure administration, together with his spite against the notorious "nationalist-socialism", played a fatal role here. In politics spite generally plays the basest of roles.

I also fear that Comrade Dzerzhinsky, who went to the Caucasus to investigate the "crime" of those "nationalist-socialists", distinguished himself there by his "genuine" Russian frame of mind (it is common knowledge that people of other nationalities who have become Russified overdo this Russian frame of mind) and that the impartiality of his whole commission was typified well enough by Orjonikidze's "manhandling". I think that no provocation or even insult can justify such Russian manhandling and that Comrade Dzerzhinsky was inexcusably guilty in adopting a light-hearted attitude towards it.

For all the citizens in the Caucasus Orjonikidze was the authority. Orjonikidze had no right to display that irritability to which he and Dzerzhinsky referred. On the contrary, Orjonikidze should have behaved with a restraint which cannot be demanded of any ordinary citizen, still less of a man accused of a "political" crime. And, to tell the truth, those nationalist-socialists were citizens who were accused of a political crime, and the terms of the accusation were such that it could not be described otherwise.

Here we have an important question of principle: how is internationalism to be understood?*

Lenin

December 30, 1922
Taken down by M. V.

---

* After this the following phrase was crossed out in the shorthand text: "It seems to me that our comrades have not studied this important question of principle sufficiently."—*Ed.*

Continuation of the notes.
December 31, 1922

THE QUESTION OF NATIONALITIES
OR "AUTONOMISATION"
(*Continued*)

In my writings on the national question I have already said
that an abstract presentation of the question of nationalism
is of no use at all. A distinction must necessarily be made
between the nationalism of an oppressor nation and that of
an opporessed nation, the nationalism of a big nation and that
of a small nation.

In respect of the second kind of nationalism we, nationals
of a big nation, have nearly always been quilty, in historic
practice, of an infinite number of cases of violence; furthermore, we commit violence and insult an infinite number of
times without noticing it. It is sufficient to recall my Volga
reminiscences[70] of how non-Russians are treated; how the
Poles are not called by any other name than Polyachishka,
how the only way to mock at a Tatar is to call him Prince,
how the Ukrainians are always Khokhols and the Georgians
and other Caucasian nationals always Kapkasians.

That is why internationalism on the part of oppressor, or
"great" nations, as they are called (though they are great only
in their violence, only great as Derzhimordas), must consist
not only in the observance of the formal equality of nations
but even in an inequality of the oppressor nation, the great
nation, that must make up for the inequality which obtains
in actual practice. Anybody who does not understand this
has not grasped the real proletarian attitude to the national
question, he is still essentially petty bourgeois in his point of

view and is, therefore, sure to descend to the bourgeois point of view.

What is important to the proletarian? To the proletarian it is not only important, it is absolutely essential that he should be assured that the non-Russians place the greatest possible trust in the proletarian class struggle. What is needed to ensure this? Not merely formal equality. In one way or another, by one's attitude or by concessions, it is necessary to compensate the non-Russians for the lack of trust, suspicion and insults to which the government of the "dominant" nation has subjected them in the past.

I think it is unnecessary to explain this to Bolsheviks, to Communists, in greater detail. And I think that in the present instance, as far as the Georgian nation is concerned, we have a typical case in which a genuinely proletarian attitude makes profound caution, thoughtfulness and a readiness to compromise a matter of necessity for us. The Georgian who is neglectful of this aspect of the question, or who carelessly flings about accusations of "nationalist-socialism" (whereas he himself is a real and true "nationalist-socialist", and even a vulgar Great-Russian Derzhimorda), violates, in substance, the interests of proletarian class solidarity, for nothing holds up the development and strengthening of proletarian class solidarity so much as national injustice; "offended" nationals are not sensitive to anything so much as to the feeling of equality and the violation of this sentiment, if only through negligence or as a joke—to the violation of that equality by their proletarian comrades. That is why in this case it is better to overdo rather than underdo concessions and leniency towards the national minorities. That is why, in this case, the fundamental interest of proletarian solidarity, and consequently of the proletarian class struggle, requires that we never adopt a formal attitude to the national question, but always take into account the specific attitude of the proletarian of the oppressed (or small) nation towards the oppressor (or great) nation.

Lenin

Taken down by M. V.

December 31, 1922

What practical measures must be taken in the present situation?

Firstly, we must maintain and strengthen the union of socialist republics. Of this there can be no doubt. This measure is necessary for us and it is necessary for the world communist proletariat in the struggle against the world bourgeoisie and in its defence against bourgeois intrigues.

Secondly, the union of socialist republics must be retained for its diplomatic apparatus. By the way, this apparatus is an exceptional component of our state apparatus. We have not allowed a single influential person from the old tsarist apparatus into it. All sections with any authority are composed of Communists. That is why it has already won for itself (this may be said boldly) the name of a reliable communist apparatus purged to an incomparably greater extent of the old tsarist, bourgeois and petty-bourgeois elements than that which we have to make do with in other People's Commissariats.

Thirdly, exemplary punishment must be inflicted on Comrade Orjonikidze (I say this all the more regretfully as I am one of his personal friends and worked with him abroad) and the investigation of all the material which Dzerzhinsky's commission has collected must be completed or started over again to correct the enormous mass of wrongs and biased judgements which it doubtlessly contains. The political responsibility for all this truly Great-Russian nationalist campaign must, of course, be laid on Stalin and Dzerzhinsky.

Fourthly, the strictest rules must be introduced on the use of the national language in the non-Russian republics of our union, and these rules must be checked with special care. There is no doubt that our apparatus being what it is, there is bound to be, on the pretext of unity in the railway service, unity in the fiscal service and so on, a mass of truly Russian abuses. Special ingenuity is necessary for the struggle against these abuses, not to mention special sincerity on the part of those who undertake that struggle. A detailed code will be required, and only the nationals living in the republic in question can draw it up at all successfully. And then we cannot be sure in advance that as a result of that work we shall not take a step backward at our next congress of Soviets, i.e., retain the union of Soviet socialist republics only for military and diplomatic affairs, and in all other respects restore full independence to the individual People's Commissariats.

It must be borne in mind that the decentralisation of the People's Commissariats and the lack of co-ordination in their work as far as Moscow and other centres are concerned can be compensated sufficiently by Party authority, if it is exercised with sufficient prudence and impartiality; the harm that can result to our state from a lack of unity between the national apparatuses and the Russian apparatus is infinitely less than that which is being done not only to us, but to the whole International, and to the hundreds of millions of the peoples of Asia, who are destined to come forward on the stage of history in the near future, following us. It would be unpardonable opportunism if we, on the eve of the debut of the East, just as it is awakening, undermined our authority with its peoples, even if only by the slightest crudity or injustice towards our own non-Russian nationalities. The necessity to rally against the imperialists of the West who are defending the capitalist world is one thing. There can be no doubt about that and it would be superfluous for me to speak about my unconditional approval of it. It is another thing when we ourselves lapse, even if only in trifles, into imperialist attitudes towards oppressed nationalities, thus undermining all our principled sincerity, all our defence on principle of the struggle against imperialism. But the morrow of world history will be the day when the awakening peoples oppressed by imperialism will be finally aroused and the decisive long, hard struggle for their liberation will begin.

Lenin

December 31, 1922

Taken down by M V.

Published in *Kommunist* No. 9 and as separate pamphlet

Collected Works, Vol. 36

BETTER FEWER, BUT BETTER

Excerpt

The system of international relationships which has now taken shape is one in which a European state, Germany, is enslaved by the victor countries. Furthermore, owing to their victory, a number of states, the oldest states in the West, are in a position to make some concessions to their oppressed classes—concessions which, insignificant though they are, nevertheless retard the revolutionary movement in those countries and create some semblance of "social peace".

At the same time, as a result of the last imperialist war, a number of countries of the East, India, China, etc., have been completely jolted out of the rut. Their development has definitely shifted to general European capitalist lines. The general European ferment has begun to affect them, and it is now clear to the whole world that they have been drawn into a process of development that must lead to a crisis in the whole of world capitalism.

Thus, at the present time we are confronted with the question—shall we be able to hold on with our small and very small peasant production, and in our present state of ruin, until the West European capitalist countries consummate their development towards socialism? But they are consummating it not as we formerly expected. They are not consummating it through the gradual "maturing" of socialism, but through the exploitation of some countries by others, through the exploitation of the first of the countries vanquished in the imperialist war combined with the exploitation of the whole of the East. On the other hand, precisely as a result of the first imperialist war, the East has been definitely drawn into the revolutionary movement, has been definitely drawn into the general maelstrom of the world revolutionary movement.

What tactics does this situation prescribe for our country? Obviously the following. We must display extreme caution so as to preserve our workers' government and to retain our small and very small peasantry under its leadership and authority. We have the advantage that the whole world is now passing to a movement that must give rise to a world socialist revolution. But we are labouring under the disadvantage that the imperialists have succeeded in splitting the world into two camps; and this split is made more complicated by the fact that it is extremely difficult for Germany, which is really a land of advanced, cultured, capitalist development, to rise to her feet. All the capitalist powers of what is called the West are pecking at her and preventing her from rising. On the other hand, the entire East, with its hundreds of millions of exploited working people reduced to the last degree of human suffering, has been forced into a position where its physical and material strength cannot possibly be compared with the physical, material and military strength of any of the much smaller West European states.

Can we save ourselves from the impending conflict with these imperialist countries? May we hope that the internal antagonisms and conflicts between the thriving imperialist countries of the West and the thriving imperialist countries of the East will give us a second respite as they did the first time, when the campaign of the West European counter-revolution in support of the Russian counter-revolution broke down owing to the antagonisms in the camp of the counter-revolutionaries of the West and the East, in the camp of the Eastern and Western exploiters, in the camp of Japan and America?

I think the reply to this question should be that the issue depends upon too many factors, and that the outcome of the struggle as a whole can be forecast only because in the long run capitalism itself is educating and training the vast majority of the population of the globe for the struggle.

In the last analysis, the outcome of the struggle will be determined by the fact that Russia, India, China, etc., account for the overwhelming majority of the population of the globe. And it is this majority that, during the past few years, has been drawn into the struggle for emancipation with extraordinary rapidity, so that in this respect there cannot be the slightest doubt what the final outcome of the world struggle will be. In this sense, the complete victory of socialism is fully and absolutely assured.

But what interests us is not the inevitability of this complete victory of socialism, but the tactics which we, the Russian Communist Party, we, the Russian Soviet Government, should pursue to prevent the West European counter-revolutionary states from crushing us. To ensure our existence until the next military conflict between the counter-revolutionary imperialist West and the revolutionary and nationalist East, between the most civilised countries of the world and the Orientally backward countries which, however, comprise the majority, this majority must become civilised. We, too, lack enough civilisation to enable us to pass straight on to socialism, although we do have the political requisites for it. We should adopt the following tactics, or pursue the following policy to save ourselves.

We must strive to build up a state in which the workers retain the leadership of the peasants, in which they retain the confidence of the peasants, and by exercising the greatest economy remove every trace of extravagance from our social relations.

We must reduce our state apparatus to the utmost degree of economy. We must banish from it all traces of extravagance, of which so much has been left over from tsarist Russia, from its bureaucratic capitalist state machine.

Will not this be a reign of peasant limitations?

No. If we see to it that the working class retains its leadership over the peasantry, we shall be able, by exercising the greatest possible economy in the economic life of our state, to use every saving we make to develop our large-scale machine industry, to develop electrification, the hydraulic extraction of peat, to complete the Volkhov power project,[71] etc.

In this, and in this alone, lies our hope. Only when we have done this will we, speaking figuratively, be able to change horses, to change from the peasant, muzhik horse of poverty, from the horse of an economy designed for a ruined peasant country, to the horse which the proletariat is seeking and must seek—the horse of large-scale machine industry, of electrification, of the Volkhov power station, etc.

Pravda No. 49, March 4, 1923

Signed: *N. Lenin*

Collected Works, Vol. 33

NOTES

[1] At the close of 1905 a revolution broke out in Persia with demonstrations against the despotic regime of the Shah, who had reduced the people to utter destitution and helped the imperialist powers to convert the country into a semi-colony.

Under an agreement between the Russian Tsar and the Shah of Persia Colonel Lyakhov's Russian Cossack brigade was sent to suppress the revolution. In June 1908, Lyakhov's brigade engineered a counter-revolutionary coup d'état in Teheran and dissolved the Majlis, which had been convened on the people's demand in October 1906. Some of the deputies were brutally killed.

The popular struggle, however, continued. In July 1909 revolutionary detachments entered Teheran, defeated Lyakhov's Cossacks and deposed Shah Mohammed Ali.

The revolution was crushed as a result of foreign imperialist intervention. The Russian Tsar and the British Government concluded an agreement on dividing Persia into Russian and British spheres of influence and in 1911 occupied a considerable part of Persian territory; they abolished the gains of the revolution and re-established the rule of the Shah and the feudals. p. 5

[2] This refers to the First Duma which the tsarist government, frightened by the revolution that had begun in Russia, was forced to convene at the end of April 1906. It was dissolved by the tsar in July 1906. p. 5

[3] The insurrection referred to is the Moscow armed uprising of December 1905 which was accompanied by workers' armed actions in other cities. That was the culmination of the Russian Revolution of 1905-07. p. 5

[4] Reference is to the defeat suffered by the tsarist army in the Russo-Japanese War of 1904-05. p. 5.

[5] *Nicholas Romanov*—the Russian Tsar Nicholas II. p. 5

[6] *Black Hundreds*—monarchist gangs formed by the tsarist police to fight against the Russian revolutionary movement. p. 5

[7] Lenin refers to the British Government. p. 6

[8] This refers to the Turkish revolution of 1908-09 against the despotic regime of Sultan Abdul Hamid II. It was led by the Young Turks, members of the Unity and Progress Party founded in 1894 by a group of progressive intellectuals representing commercial interests.

In July 1908, troops commanded by Young Turk officers mutinied and were supported by the townsfolk and peasants. Fearing the spread of the revolutionary movement, Sultan Abdul Hamid II agreed to restore the Constitution of 1876, which he had himself abrogated in 1878 when he dissolved parliament. A new parliament was convened at the end of 1908.

In April 1909, the Sultan attempted a counter-revolutionary putsch in Constantinople, but after two days of street fighting the Young Turks won a victory, deposed Abdul Hamid II and proclaimed Turkey a constitutional monarchy. A new, Young Turk, government was formed. p. 6

[9] The reference is to Sultan Abdul Hamid II. p. 6

[10] *Morley, John* (1838-1923)—British political figure and author; a leader of the Liberal Party; Secretary of State for India, 1906-10. p. 7

[11] *Cadets*—members of the *Constitutional-Democratic Party*, the political party of the liberal-monarchist bourgeoisie in Russia. p. 7

[12] *Genghis Khan* (about 1155-1227)—Mongolian conqueror, who seized Siberia, North China, Central Asia, Northern Iran and other lands. His army ravaged the conquered countries and exterminated the population. p. 7

[13] *Plehve, V. K.* (1846-1904)—reactionary statesman in tsarist Russia, chief of gendarmes; organised brutal reprisals against revolutionary workers and peasants. p. 7

[14] *Tilak Balgangadkhar* (1850-1920)—Indian revolutionary; fought against the British colonialists for Indian independence. p. 7

[15] *Sun Yat-sen* (1866-1925)—great Chinese revolutionary and democrat; after the October Revolution friend of Soviet Russia. p. 9

[16] In the spring of 1911 a revolution developed in China; the Manchu dynasty was overthrown and China was proclaimed a republic. Dr. Sun Yat-sen who led the revolutionary movement was elected provisional President of the Chinese Republic. However, under pressure from the counter-revolutionary forces he was compelled to resign in favour of Yüan Shih-k'ai, an adventurist who established a counter-revolutionary military dictatorship. p. 9

[17] *Narodnik*—supporter of the ideological and political trend which arose in Russia in the seventies of the nineteenth century. The distinctive features of the Narodnik ideology were the denial of the leading role of the working class in the revolutionary movement and the erroneous belief that a socialist revolution could be effected by the peasantry, i.e., small proprietors. The Narodniks saw in the Russian village commune a germ of socialism, though actually it was a survival of feudalism and serfdom. Theirs was a utopian socialism far removed from actual social development. It was merely a phrase, a dream or good wish. p. 9

[18] *Herzen, Alexander Ivanovich* (1812-1870)–Russian revolutionary democrat and writer; beginning with 1857 published the magazine *Kolokol (The Bell)* in London, which was illegally transported to Russia where it played an important part in developing the revolutionary movement. p. 10

[19] *The Peasant Union*–a revolutionary-democratic peasant organisation in Russia in 1905-06. p. 10

[20] *Trudoviks*–a group of petty-bourgeois democrats in the Russian Duma, consisting mainly of peasants. The Trudovik Group was constituted in April 1906 from the peasant deputies to the First Duma. p. 10.

[21] *The State Duma*–a representative body in tsarist Russia, which the tsar was forced to convene as a result of the 1905-07 revolution. It was formally a legislative body, but possessed no real power. The elections to the Duma were indirect and unequal and were not universal. The franchise of the working people and the non-Russian nationalities inhabiting Russia was greatly curtailed and a considerable section of the workers and peasants had no franchise whatever.

The First Duma (April-July 1906) and the Second Duma (February-June 1907) were dissolved by the tsarist government. The Third Duma (1907-12) and the Fourth Duma (1912-17) were dominated by a reactionary bloc of landowners and big capitalists, supporters of the autocracy. p. 10

[22] The reference is to the leaders of the French Revolution of 1789-94. p. 11

[23] *Yüan Shih-k'ai* (1859-1916)–Chinese statesman; before the 1911 revolution served under the Manchu dynasty; in 1912 he was elected President of the Chinese Republic and later established a counter-revolutionary dictatorship. p. 11

[24] *George, Henry* (1839-1897)–American petty-bourgeois economist and author; considered landed proprietorship to be the chief cause of the bad condition of the working people, and asserted that nationalisation of land or high ground rent could put an end to poverty and want in bourgeois society. p. 13

[25] In September 1911, Italy attacked Tripoli and Cyrenaica in North Africa, then part of the Ottoman Empire. The weak Turkish garrisons were soon crushed, but for many months the Italians had to contend with the courageous resistance of the Arab population. The war ended in the victory of the Italian imperialists. p. 16

[5] This refers to the first Russian Revolution of 1905-07. p. 22

[7] *Derzhimorda*–the name of a policeman in Gogol's *Inspector-General*, a boorish, brutal oppressor, a man of violence. p. 22

[8] *Purishkevich, V. M.* (1870-1920)–Russian landowner, rabid reactionary and monarchist. p. 24

[9] *The Lena Goldfields* in Siberia were owned by British capitalists in partnership with Russian capitalists, among them members of the

tsar's family. On April 4 (17), 1912, tsarist gendarmes opened fire on an unarmed demonstration of strikers, killing 270 and wounding 250 workers.

In answer to the bloody events in the Lena Goldfields a wave of protest meetings, strikes and demonstrations involving hundreds of thousands of workers swept over the country.   p. 25

³⁰ Narodnik ideas (see Note 17) were supported by the petty-bourgeois parties of Socialist-Revolutionaries and Popular Socialists.   p. 28

³¹ *Menshikov, M. O.* (1859-1919)–Russian reactionary writer, monarchist.   p. 28

³² These are names of Russian opportunist Social-Democrats (Mensheviks), anarchists and Socialist-Revolutionaries who betrayed socialism and went over to the side of the tsarist government. In 1914, when the First World War broke out, they came out in support of the imperialist war and the annexationist policy of Russian tsarism.

                                                                         p. 28

³³ *The Council of the United Nobility*–an organisation of feudal-minded landowners, supporters of the autocracy; fought against the revolutionary movement in Russia.   p. 29

³⁴ Here Lenin gives the names of representatives of the big commercial and industrial bourgeoisie, members of the Octobrist and Cadet parties.   p. 29

³⁵ *Radishchev, Alexander Nikolayevich* (1749-1802)–Russian writer, revolutionary enlightener, author of the book *Journey from Petersburg to Moscow* (1790) in which he exposed the autocracy and demanded the abolition of serfdom in Russia. The tsarist government sentenced him to death for the book; the sentence was commuted to exile to Siberia.   p. 29

³⁶ *Decembrists*–Russian revolutionaries, members of the nobility, who on December 14, 1825, raised a revolt against the autocracy. The revolt was suppressed by tsarist troops. Five leaders of the Decembrists were executed and others banished to exile in Siberia.
                                                                         p. 29

³⁷ *The revolutionary commoners of the 1870s* were participants in the revolutionary movement. They carried on revolutionary propaganda among the peasantry and fought against the autocracy by terrorist methods.   p. 29.

³⁸ *Chernyshevsky, Nikolai Gavrilovich* (1828-1889)–Russian revolutionary democrat, materialist philosopher and writer, leader of the revolutionary-democratic movement of the 1850-1860s in Russia. In 1862 he was arrested by the tsarist government and sentenced to penal servitude in Siberia.   p. 29

³⁹ Quoted from N. G. Chernyshevsky's *Prologue*.   p. 29

⁴⁰ *Romanovs*–dynasty of Russian tsars.
       Bobrinsky and *Purishkevich*–big landowners, ultra-reactionaries and monarchists.   p. 30

[41] Lassalleans—supporters and followers of Ferdinand Lassalle, a German petty-bourgeois socialist. Marx and Engels called them "Royal-Prussian socialists" because they preached the introduction of socialism into Prussia with the help of the Prussian royal government, headed by Bismarck. After Bismarck promised to carry out some reforms, they ceased their struggle against the Prussian monarchy and the landed aristocracy. Marx and Engels sharply criticised the Lassalleans for this betrayal of the cause of the working class. p. 31

[42] Junkers—members of the Prussian landed aristocracy. They provided the reactionary bureaucracy that ruled the Kingdom of Prussia and the nationalist-minded and militarist officer corps of the Prussian army. p. 31

[43] Prior to 1871 Germany was divided into many separate states. The unification of the German states under the supremacy of Prussia was undertaken by Bismarck, Chancellor of Prussia, who effected it by means of violence and wars (the Prusso-Danish War of 1864 for Schleswig-Holstein, the Austro-Prussian War of 1866). After the victory won by Prussia in the Franco-Prussian War of 1870-71, twenty-five German states were united to form the German Empire. Wilhelm I of Prussia was proclaimed German Emperor. p. 31

[44] The wars referred to are those waged by revolutionary France beginning from 1792 against the counter-revolutionary coalition of European autocratic states that tried to crush the revolution by force of arms; they also include the wars waged by Napoleon. p. 34

[45] The Franco-Prussian War (1870-71) ended in the defeat of France. p. 34

[46] Liebknecht, Wilhelm (1826-1900)—leader of the German working-class movement for many years, one of the founders of the German Social-Democratic Party, comrade-in-arms of Marx and Engels. p. 34

[47] The Entente Cordiale—military alliance of Britain, France and Russia, formed in the decade preceding the First World War; in 1915 it was joined by Japan. p. 39

[48] Economism—an opportunist trend in Russian Social-Democracy at the turn of the century. The Economists limited the tasks of the working class to the economic struggle for higher wages, better working conditions, etc., asserting that the political struggle was the business of the liberal bourgeoisie. They denied the leading role of the party of the working class and belittled the significance of revolutionary theory, declaring that the working-class movement had to develop spontaneously. Lenin exposed the inconsistency and harmfulness of Economism in his book What Is To Be Done? p. 41

[49] Alexinsky, G. A. (b.1879)—Social-Democrat, belonged to the "otzovists" who demanded the recall of Social-Democratic deputies from the Duma; subsequently a monarchist and counter-revolutionary. p. 42

[50] *Lensch, Paul* (1873-1926) and *Cunow, Heinrich* (1862-1936)–ideologists of the extreme Right wing of the German Social-Democratic Party which supported the colonial policy of the German imperialists. p. 43

[51] *Suzdal daubing*–work done in a crude primitive fashion. The expression originally referred to the cheap, gaudily painted icons made in Suzdal Uyezd before the Revolution. p. 47

[52] Lenin's *Message to the Indian Revolutionary Association* was transmitted by radio. It was a reply to a resolution adopted on March 4, 1920, by a rally of Indian revolutionaries and forwarded to Lenin. It expressed profound gratitude to Soviet Russia for its historic struggle to liberate the oppressed classes and nations. p. 50

[53] *Roy, Manabendra Nath* (1892-1948)–Indian political figure, in 1910-15 participated in the revolutionary movement against British colonialists in India; in 1915 left India for Mexico where he lived until 1920; he joined the communist movement and was delegated to the second, third, fourth and fifth congresses of the Communist International; from 1924 on was member of the Executive Committee of the Comintern; subsequently left the ranks of the Communist movement and from 1940 headed the Radical-Democratic People's Party of India. p. 51

[54] *The Second International*–an international association of socialist parties founded in 1889. When the First World War broke out, its leaders betrayed socialism and went over to the side of their own imperialist governments. The Second International collapsed. The Left parties and groups formerly affiliated to the Second International joined the Communist Third International, founded in Moscow in 1919. The Second International was re-established in 1919 at a conference in Berne (Switzerland). Only the opportunist, Right-wing Socialist parties joined it. p. 51

[55] *The Basle Manifesto* was adopted by the Basle Congress of the Second International held in November 1912. The manifesto called on socialists in all countries to "prevent the outbreak of war" and declared that "the proletariat considers it a crime to shoot at its brothers for the sake of the profits of the capitalists, the ambitions of the dynasties or the secret treaties of the diplomats". Should war break out, "socialists must intervene to achieve its speedy termination and exploit the economic and political crisis created by the war to rouse the people and thereby hasten the collapse of capitalist domination".

When the First World War did break out in July 1914 most of the Second International leaders betrayed socialism, renounced the Basle resolution and sided with their imperialist governments. p. 56

[56] *Pravda (The Truth)*–a daily newspaper, organ of the Central Committee of the C.P.S.U.; began publication in St. Petersburg on April 22 (May 5), 1912. p. 57

[57] *Iskra (The Spark)*—the first All-Russia illegal Marxist newspaper; was founded by Lenin abroad in December 1900 from where it was illegally transported to Russia. It played a tremendous part in fostering ideological unity among Russian Social-Democrats and laid the foundation for the welding of scattered local organisations into a revolutionary Marxist party.

The name "old *Iskra*" was used to distinguish it from the "new", Menshevik, *Iskra* of 1903-05. p. 57

[58] *The Two-and-a-Half International*—an international association founded in Vienna in 1921 at a conference of Centrist parties and groups which, under pressure of the revolutionary-minded working masses, temporarily seceded from the Second International but returned to it in 1923. p. 57

[59] *Spengler, Oswald* (1880-1936)—German reactionary author and idealist philosopher, depicted the decay of culture in capitalist society as the decay of world culture in general. p. 58

[60] The Russian Social-Democratic Labour Party was founded in July 1903 at the congress of representatives from all Social-Democratic organisations in Russia. It began in Brussels and continued in London. p. 58

[61] Reference is to the cash contributions made by workers for the publication of *Pravda* in tsarist Russia. p. 58

[62] *The Second All-Russia Congress of Soviets of Workers' and Soldiers' Deputies* held in Petrograd on October 25 (November 7), 1917, proclaimed that power had passed into the hands of the Soviets of Workers', Soldiers' and Peasants' Deputies, and formed the first Soviet Government. p. 59

[63] In March 1922, a workers uprising broke out in South Africa. The reactionary government of General Smuts used artillery, tanks and aircraft against the insurgents, and the uprising was put down on March 14. Hundreds of workers were killed and thousands court-martialled. The young Communist Party of South Africa took an active part in the revolt, many of its members dying heroically in the fighting. p. 59

[64] *Chartism*—the first mass movement of the working class; it developed in Britain in the 30s-40s of the nineteenth century. Its participants published the People's Charter (hence the name of the movement) and fought for the political demands it contained—universal suffrage, no land property qualifications for deputies to Parliament, etc. Meetings and demonstrations, involving millions of workers and handicraftsmen, were held all over the country for many years.

In April 1848 the Third National Convention of the Chartists drafted a petition to be presented to Parliament; it was signed by over five million people. However, the British Parliament, the overwhelming majority in which were representatives of the landed aristocracy and big bourgeoisie, refused to grant the People's

Charter and rejected all petitions. The government carried out brutal reprisals against the Chartists—their leaders were arrested and the movement was suppressed, but chartism had a great influence on the development of the international working-class movement. p.59

65 *Henderson, Arthur* (1863-1935)—one of the opportunist leaders of the British labour movement, who sided with the bourgeoisie; several times member of the British Government. p. 59

66 *Varlin, Louis Eugène* (1839-1871)—French revolutionary, outstanding leader of the Paris Commune of 1871, was executed by the Versailles troops in May 1871. *Renaudel, Pierre* (1871-1935)—French Right Socialist; during the First World War supported the imperialist policy of the French Government. p. 59

67 *Bebel, August* (1840-1913)—one of the founders and leaders of the German Social-Democratic Party, comrade-in-arms of Marx and Engels. *Südekum, Albert* (1871-1944), *Scheidemann, Philipp* (1865-1939), *Noske, Gustav* (1868-1946)—German Right-wing Social-Democrats, traitors to the working class; took part in suppressing the revolutionary working-class movement. p. 59

68 *Autonomisation*—reference is to the suggestion that the Soviet republics be united by joining the R.S.F.S.R. as autonomous units. The "autonomisation" draft was proposed by Stalin. Lenin subjected the draft to serious criticism. He proposed a fundamentally different solution—voluntary unification of all the Soviet republics in a Union of Soviet Socialist Republics, in which each member would enjoy full equality. The First All-Union Congress of Soviets in December 1922 adopted a decision to form the Union of Soviet Socialist Republics. p. 61

69 This refers to the conflict between the Transcaucasian Regional Committee of the R.C.P. (B) headed by Orjonikidze and the Mdivani group in the Communist Party of Georgia. p. 61

70 V. I. Lenin was born in Simbirsk (now Ulyanovsk) on the Volga, and spent there his childhood and youth. p. 64

71 *Volkhov power project*—big power project on the River Volkhov, the first to be undertaken by the Soviet Union. Construction began in 1918, but was fully developed only in 1921, after the Civil War. The Volkhov power plant was commissioned in 1926. p. 70